Dr Gareth Moore is the author of over 40 brain training and puzzle books for both children and adults, including *The Mammoth Book of Fun Brain Training*, *The Mammoth Book of New Sudoku*, and *The Mammoth Book of Brain Workouts*. His puzzles have also appeared in a wide range of newspapers and magazines.

He created the brain training website *BrainedUp.com*, and runs the popular online puzzle site *PuzzleMix.com*.

He gained his Ph.D at the University of Cambridge, UK, in the field of machine intelligence, teaching computers to understand human speech.

More information about him can be found at his website, *DrGarethMoore.com*.

Also available

The Mammoth Book of

Brain Games

Dr. Gareth Moore

ROBINSON

RUNNING PRESS
PHILADELPHIA · LONDON

Constable & Robinson Ltd.
55–56 Russell Square
London WC1B 4HP
www.constablerobinson.com

First published in the UK by Robinson,
an imprint of Constable & Robinson Ltd., 2014

A copy of the British Library Cataloguing in Publication Data is available from the British Library

UK ISBN: 978-1-47211-185-2 (paperback)
UK ISBN: 978-1-47211-187-6 (ebook)

1 3 5 7 9 10 8 6 4 2

First published in the United States in 2014 by Running Press Book Publishers,
A Member of the Perseus Books Group

Books published by Running Press are available at special discounts for bulk purchases in the
United States by corporations, institutions, and other organizations. For more information,
please contact the Special Markets Department at the Perseus Books Group,
2300 Chestnut Street, Suite 200, Philadelphia, PA 19103, or call (800) 810-4145, ext. 5000, or
e-mail special.markets@perseusbooks.com.

US ISBN: 978-0-7624-5226-2
US Library of Congress Control Number: 2014931280

9 8 7 6 5 4 3 2 1
Digit on the right indicates the number of this printing

Running Press Book Publishers
2300 Chestnut Street
Philadelphia, PA 19103-4371
Visit us on the web!
www.runningpress.com

Printed and bound by CPI Group (UK) Ltd, Croydon, CR0 4YY

CONTENTS

Weeks 2 to 51:
*Calculate the page number of the first day of
each week by taking the week number and
adding a 1 on the end. This is a brain games
book after all!*

INTRODUCTION

Welcome to *The Mammoth Book of Brain Games*, packed from cover to cover with an entire year's worth of puzzles and brain teasers.

There are 52 weeks of content in this book, each containing seven days of material. The first six days of each week feature either a logic puzzle, an observation puzzle, a number puzzle or a word puzzle, and then on the final day there's a Re-Thinking page which challenges you to make better use of your brain in your daily life. These cover a huge range of topics throughout the year, containing many examples of just how amazing your brain is, as well as a selection of practical tips to put to use in your daily life.

Brain Games Variety

Your brain thrives on novelty, so this book sets out to give you just that, with an exceptionally wide range of content. There are 78 entirely different types of puzzle, none of which repeat even once within 13 weeks of each other.

The book is designed to be worked through in order, so I suggest you start at the beginning and follow through. Each puzzle is assigned a category, such as Reasoning, Concentration or Speed, and you won't find the same category of puzzle on two consecutive days. Puzzles of the same type are arranged in order of increasing difficulty, so for example the hardest puzzles are in the final quarter of the book.

Start by reading the introductory text above a puzzle, then read the full instructions at the bottom before starting on the puzzle itself. Even on types where you are sure you know what to do, sometimes there are time limits or other additional rules in the instructions section. Some puzzles have example solutions to help clarify the rules, but if there's no example then take a quick peek at the solutions to work out how the puzzle works, if you need to.

Introduction

Brain Points

Each puzzle has a number of brain points to be scored for its successful completion, so, if you wish to keep track of your progress, you can use the instructions at the head of each puzzle page to calculate your score for that puzzle. There are also boxes at the foot of every puzzle page to keep track of your running total, and at the end of each week there is a space to convert your brain points into a brain rank. It's good to be able to see the progress you're making.

Solutions are given at the end of each week, with the first three days on one page and the second three days on the next. It's best to wait until you complete the third or sixth day of a week before scoring yourself and viewing the solutions, otherwise it will be all too easy to glimpse the solution to the following day's puzzle.

When scoring yourself, use the rule at the top of the puzzle page as a guideline but feel free to amend it if you wish. Where a scoring rule asks you to count incorrect squares or clues, the intention is for you to count both incorrect *and* unsolved squares or clues towards this total. You should also never score yourself less than 5 points for any page you try, and similarly don't award yourself more than the total number of points given on that page – even if the scoring formula would otherwise allow you to score more, which it quite often does. If unsure, award yourself what you consider a fair share of the points for your achievement on that puzzle.

Brain Rank

On the final page of each week you'll find a space to write your current "Brain Rank". You can find this by looking up your current number of Brain Points in the conversion chart on pages 531-533.

The aim of the Brain Rank is to encourage you to keep pushing your brain just that little bit further, turning an abstract number into a friendly label. The precise description of each Brain Rank is for fun only, but they are generally indicative of your progress to date.

Introduction

Puzzle Difficulty

Each puzzle is designed to stand alone from all the others, and of course you're certain to find some types harder than others. The number of points available per puzzle is intended to reflect the relative difficulty of the puzzle, but your precise performance on each puzzle will naturally also depend on your prior experience. For example, if you've never solved a cryptic crossword before then you might well find it extremely difficult to collect many of the brain points for that puzzle – whereas an existing expert might breeze through it.

There are some hints in the Re-Thinking sections to help you tackle tougher puzzles, but in general don't be afraid to take a guess and see what happens. It's a perfectly valid learning technique, and in the worst case you'll be exactly where you were already!

Your Brain Schedule

There's no need to precisely match the weeks and days in the book to calendar weeks and days, but for maximum brain benefit it's best to aim to complete a week of content in around a week of real time. Try to make the book a regular part of your day, if you can, and if you can minimize distractions while solving then you'll reap the best mental benefits.

At the start of each week is a space to write the date you began that week, and then at the end is a space to write your completion date. These help you keep track of your progress.

International English

All of the word puzzles are designed for all English speakers, so whatever version of English you use, whether you hail from the US, the UK, Australia or indeed anywhere else, you can be sure that there won't be any word clues that require you to use spellings you don't normally use, or call upon knowledge you're unlikely to have.

Introduction

Your Opinion Matters

If you have any feedback on this book, either good or bad, please don't hesitate to get in touch. I personally wrote all of the puzzles and text in this book, and it's always helpful to hear what people enjoy the most, or which puzzles they find too easy or too hard. I'm always happy to receive email to braingames@drgarethmoore.com.

Further Brain Training Material

If you're looking to augment your brain training regime with additional tasks, there are plenty of ideas spread throughout the book in the Re-Thinking sections. These range from exercises to improve your memory through to ways to unleash your creativity and powers of imagination, which in turn can help you think smarter thoughts!

For daily material, my brain training website at BrainedUp.com provides a range of interactive tasks that perfectly complement the more in-depth challenges in this book. The content automatically adjusts to your skill on each task, continually challenging you at just the right level to keep your brain learning without becoming frustratingly difficult.

If you particularly enjoy the logic puzzles, you can find more of these on my online puzzle site at PuzzleMix.com. There are new puzzles every day, and you can discuss the puzzles and choose to compare your solving times with other users if you wish to.

Last, but not least, pages 541 to 544 at the very back of this book contain details of some of my other brain training and puzzle books.

Good luck, and enjoy the brain training!

Dr Gareth Moore, January 2014

For my parents,
for their love and support

Week 1

Total Brain Points Available: **125**

Reasoning
MINESWEEPER

The classic game, as supplied with Windows™. This version can be solved using logic alone – no guessing is required!

1			0				
1			1			0	
	0						0
		0	3			0	
	3		3				
	5				3		1
						2	
	3	2	2	2		2	

Instructions

☐ Find the hidden mines in the grid.
☐ Mines can only be placed in empty grid squares.
☐ A number in a square reveals the number of
  touching mines, including diagonally.

Language

CROSSWORD

Across

2 At the highest point (4)
4 Blood fluid (6)
6 Burst (4)
8 Smoke deposit (4)
10 Married title (3)
11 Defrauded (7)
13 Large, flightless bird (7)
16 Clod (3)
17 Warmth (4)
18 Scary feeling (4)
20 Went out (6)

Down

1 Mayhem (5)
2 Large primate (3)
3 Oppressed (10)
4 Sited (10)
5 'Mamma Mia' songwriters (4)
7 Searched for in Iraq (inits) (3)
9 Not that, but ___ (4)
12 Engrave (4)
13 Not on (3)
14 Infrequent (4)
15 Sizeable (5)

Number Skills

BRAIN CHAINS

Without using a calculator or making any written notes, solve each brain chain as quickly as you can.

| **44** | ÷4 | -3 | ×10 | ÷2 | -10 | RESULT |

| **13** | -3 | ×3 | +60% | ×1/2 | -50% | RESULT |

| **40** | ×1/2 | +5 | +80% | ×2/5 | ÷6 | RESULT |

Instructions

☐ Start with the bold value on the left of the chain.
☐ Follow the arrow and apply the first operation. Remember the resulting value in your head.
☐ Follow the next arrow and apply the second operation to the value you remembered.
☐ Keep following arrows and applying operations until you reach the RESULT box. Write in the calculated value.

Speed
SPINNING LETTERS

How many words can you make from these letters in just three minutes?

There are over 50 to be found.

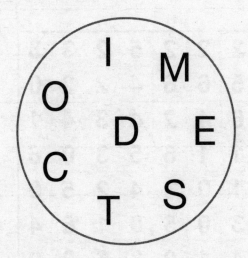

Instructions

- ☐ Make a word by using the middle letter plus any selection of the other letters, each used no more than once per word.
- ☐ Every word must be at least three letters in length, and must be a regular English word – proper nouns are not allowed.
- ☐ If you don't get anywhere near 50 words in three minutes, you can always give yourself as much extra time as you need.

Concentration

DOMINO SET

This game is not logically difficult but it requires concentration to solve, to keep track of your progress cleanly in order that you don't miss any "obvious" deductions.

0	1	2	3	4	5	6	
							0
							1
							2
							3
							4
							5
							6

6	2	2	2	5	2	3	3
1	5	6	6	4	2	2	0
4	6	4	2	4	3	4	1
1	1	1	6	5	3	0	6
5	1	0	3	4	2	5	0
5	3	0	5	0	1	6	4
5	4	1	0	3	6	3	0

Instructions

☐ Draw solid lines to divide the grid up to form a complete set of standard dominoes, with one of each domino.

☐ A '0' represents a blank on a traditional domino.

☐ Use the check-off list to help you keep track of which dominoes you've placed.

6	0	0	4	2	1	5	4
3	5	2	6	0	4	2	1
2	5	3	2	0	1	4	4
1	6	0	2	0	1	2	1
1	3	3	5	3	5	5	3
6	6	6	6	2	0	6	4
1	0	4	5	3	3	5	4

Reasoning
FENCE POSTS

It looks fairly easy to join all these dots into a loop, but it might prove trickier than it seems.

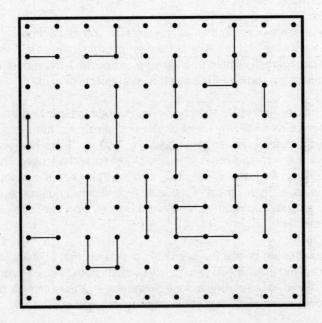

Instructions

- ☐ Join all of the dots to form a single loop.
- ☐ The loop cannot cross or touch itself at any point.
- ☐ Only horizontal and vertical lines between dots are allowed.
- ☐ Some parts of the loop are already given.

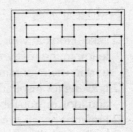

Re-Thinking
BRAIN TRAINING

Brain Training is the idea that practising one activity can make you better at other, seemingly unrelated, activities – so-called "deep transfer" of skills.

There is plenty of evidence that making sure you make thorough use of your thinking abilities is important for good brain health. A broad range of experiences help provide your brain with extra redundancy that can lessen some of the natural mental effects of aging.

What no one knows for sure, however, is which are the best activities to follow. Given this, the safest choice is to give your mind as wide a range of mental challenges as possible. That's why this book is packed with a record-breaking range of just such challenges. There are six days of puzzles each week, with a whole year of puzzles, and there is *not a single repeat* of a puzzle type within a quarter of a year. So the puzzles you've already solved this week won't be repeated for three months!

This book could be just the beginning of your mental odyssey. Why not make the time, if you can, to read a challenging book (if you aren't already), learn about a foreign country – or even learn a new language – or to challenge yourself in any other way.

Instructions

- ☐ Take a look at your life. How many new things did you do, or learn, in the past week? If the answer is none, find something new to start in the coming week.
- ☐ Looking for inspiration? If you like crafts, then get a piece of paper and look on YouTube for Origami tutorials to follow.
- ☐ Prefer physical activity? Get some juggling balls (or fruit!) and learn to juggle.
- ☐ Like music? Can you whistle a tune? Practise until you can!

Week 1 Solutions

Mark your answers using these reference solutions. Don't score less than 5 brain points for any task which you tried, and also don't score more than the given brain points total.

Day 1

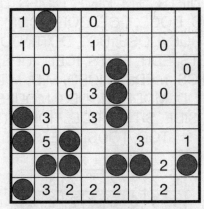

Day 2

Day 3

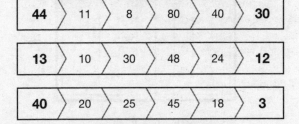

Week 1 Solutions

Day 4

Possible words include: CITED, COD, CODE, CODES, CODS, COSTED, DEISM, DEMIST, DICE, DICES, DIE, DIES, DIET, DIETS, DIM, DIME, DIMES, DIMS, DISC, DISCO, DOC, DOCS, DOE, DOES, DOME, DOMES, DOMESTIC, DOS, DOSE, DOT, DOTE, DOTES, DOTS, EDICT, EDICTS, EDIT, EDITS, ICED, IDES, IDS, MED, MEDIC, MEDICS, MEDS, MICED, MID, MIDST, MISDO, MISTED, MOD, MODE, MODES, MODEST, MODS, ODE, ODES, SIDE, SITED, TIDE, TIDES, TIED, TIMED, TOD, TODS, TOED

Day 5

6	2	2	2	5	2	3	3
1	5	6	6	4	2	2	0
4	6	4	2	4	3	4	1
1	1	1	6	5	3	0	6
5	1	0	3	4	2	5	0
5	3	0	5	0	1	6	4
5	4	1	0	3	6	3	0

Day 6

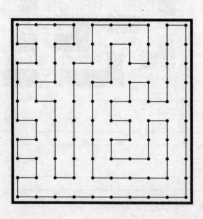

Week 2

Total Brain Points Available: **135**

Reasoning
FUTOSHIKI

These puzzles combine inequalities with Latin Squares.

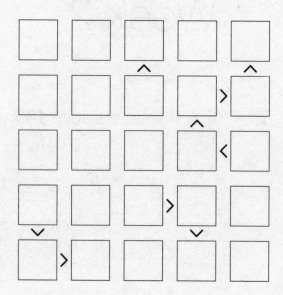

Instructions

☐ Place 1 to 5 once each into every row and column while obeying the inequality signs.

☐ Less than ("<") and greater than (">") signs between some squares indicate that the values in these two squares must be greater than or less than one another as indicated by the sign. The sign always points towards the smaller number.

Language

WORD PYRAMID

Can you build this pyramid of letter bricks using your anagram skills?

1

2

3

4

5

6

1. Canine
2. Precious metal
3. Rustic accommodation
4. Yearned
5. Sat around idly
6. Hit with a club

Instructions

☐ Each row of bricks uses the same letters as the row above it except for the addition of one extra letter. The letters may be rearranged, however, so KIT can be on the row above TICK.

☐ Solve the clues to help you fill the pyramid.

Concentration
NO 4 IN A ROW

This puzzle is a tougher, solo version of noughts and crosses.

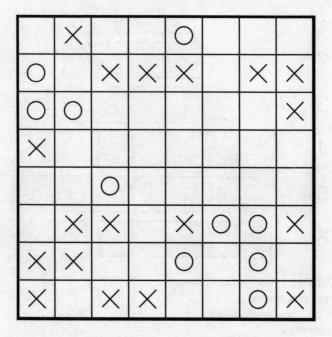

Instructions

☐ Fill the empty squares in the grid with either an 'X' or an 'O' such that no line of four consecutive 'X's or 'O's is made in any direction, including diagonally.

Observation
MATCHING PAIRS

Instructions

☐ A set of objects have been split in two, and the various resulting half-objects are shown above.

☐ Can you pair each object with its other half?

Speed

WORDSEARCH

How many of the listed films can you find in this grid within three minutes? They can be written in any direction, either forwards or backwards.

Popular Films

O	S	C	H	I	N	D	L	E	R	S	L	I	S	T
A	E	I	R	L	E	T	T	R	T	T	N	O	C	R
C	M	T	E	I	I	L	W	U	S	O	O	U	A	E
G	I	Y	A	W	A	D	E	T	I	R	I	P	S	H
O	T	L	R	G	R	O	L	U	N	R	T	M	A	T
O	N	I	W	O	U	G	V	F	A	O	C	U	B	A
D	R	G	I	T	M	F	E	E	I	T	I	G	L	F
F	E	H	N	N	A	O	A	H	P	A	F	T	A	D
E	D	T	D	E	S	Y	N	T	E	N	P	S	N	O
L	O	S	O	M	N	T	G	O	H	I	L	E	C	G
L	M	H	W	E	E	I	R	T	T	M	U	R	A	E
A	W	O	C	M	V	C	Y	K	E	R	P	R	E	H
S	N	R	B	Y	E	L	M	C	N	E	N	O	I	T
L	I	F	E	I	S	B	E	A	U	T	I	F	U	L
N	E	I	L	A	R	P	N	B	T	L	E	O	N	N

ALIEN	LEON	SCHINDLER'S LIST
BACK TO THE FUTURE	LIFE IS BEAUTIFUL	SEVEN SAMURAI
CASABLANCA	MEMENTO	SPIRITED AWAY
CITY LIGHTS	MODERN TIMES	TERMINATOR
CITY OF GOD	PSYCHO	THE GODFATHER
FORREST GUMP	PULP FICTION	THE PIANIST
GOODFELLAS	REAR WINDOW	TWELVE ANGRY MEN

Reasoning
LIGHT UP

This Japanese logic puzzle is also known as 'Akari'.

Instructions

☐ Place light bulbs in white squares so that all of the white squares either contain a bulb or are lit by at least one bulb.

☐ Light bulbs illuminate all squares in the same row and column up to the first black square encountered in each direction.

☐ No light bulb may illuminate any other light bulb.

☐ Black squares with numbers indicate how many light bulbs are placed in the touching squares (above/below/left/right).

☐ Not all light bulbs are necessarily clued.

Re-Thinking

PRIORITIES

Chances are that you don't have enough time in the day to get everything you want done. There are so many things you'd like to do if only you could find the time, and maybe even a whole host of things you've actually started but simply never finished.

Often the challenge is just getting started, either at all or to continue a suspended task. The weight of things to do can push us into inertia, so start by making a list. Write out everything you would like to do. Getting it out of your head is cleansing, and you won't need to remember every detail any more.

Now look at that list, and see if you can break it down. Smaller tasks can be more manageable.

Once you have your tasks, or sub-tasks, work out how much time you think it would take you to complete each task. Assign priorities from 1 (important to do) to 10 (not important) to each task. Maybe there are some quick, high priority tasks. Make a conscious decision to do these next time you have time, rather than getting caught in indecision.

Instructions

☐ List five tasks you'd like to complete in the coming month or two.
☐ For each task, how long do you think it would take to complete?
☐ Number them in order of priority.
☐ Decide when you would like to have completed the first task by. Set yourself a deadline.
☐ Stick the list somewhere you will regularly see it!

Day 1

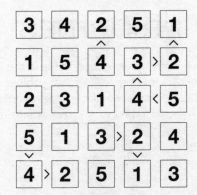

Day 2

DOG

GOLD

LODGE

LONGED

LOUNGED

BLUDGEON

Day 3

Week 2 Solutions

Day 4

Day 5

Day 6

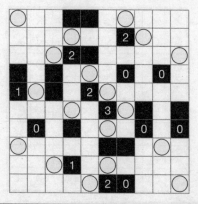

Week 3

Total Brain Points Available: **130**

Reasoning

YAJILIN

This Japanese logic puzzle combines route-finding with logical deductions based on the given clues.

Instructions

- ☐ Draw a single loop using only horizontal and vertical lines such that the loop does not pass through any square more than once.

- ☐ Any squares which the loop does not visit must be shaded, but none of these shaded squares can touch in either a horizontal or vertical direction.
- ☐ Numbers with arrows indicate the exact number of shaded squares in a given direction in a specific row or column, but not all shaded squares are necessarily identified with arrows.

Language
DELETED PAIRS

How quickly can you identify each of these concealed words?

EF AE TS LY

PM IE AR HS

RP IL EG EG NO NO

LM NO NO PK LE EY

Instructions

☐ Delete one letter from each pair so that each line spells out a word. For example: D̶E FO̶ G̶J to spell out **DOG**.

Number Skills
NUMBER PATH

Fill in the empty squares in this grid to reveal a hidden path.

100				88	87				83
	98	93					78	79	
	3	92					73	80	
				43	50				
8			41	44	49	52			69
9			40	45	48	53			68
				46	47				
	12	17					32	61	
	19	18					31	62	
21				25	26				64

Instructions

- ☐ Fill empty squares so that the completed grid contains every number from 1 to 100 exactly once each.
- ☐ Place the numbers so that there is a route from 1 to 100 that visits every grid square exactly once each in increasing numerical order, moving only left, right, up or down between touching squares.

Observation
JIGSAW CUT

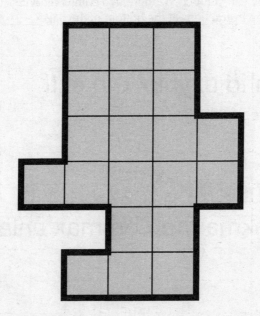

Instructions

- ☐ Draw along the existing lines to divide this shape up into four identical jigsaw pieces, with no pieces left over.
- ☐ The pieces may be rotated versions of one another, but you cannot mirror or 'turn over' any of the pieces.

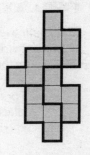

Speed
CRYPTOGRAM

How quickly can you decode these two common sayings by
following the instructions at the bottom of the page?

1. Ehhd uxyhkx rhn exti

**2. T ubkw bg max atgw bl
phkma mph bg max unla**

Instructions

☐ Both phrases have been encrypted using the same code.
☐ Each letter has been replaced with another letter a fixed number
of places forward/backward in the alphabet, wrapping around
from Z to A. The number of places shifted is the same for all
letters. For example, A might be replaced with C; B replaced with
D; C replaced with E; and so on, until X is replaced with Z; Y is
replaced with A; and Z is replaced with B.

Reasoning
RECTANGLES

This Japanese logic puzzle is also known as Shikaku.

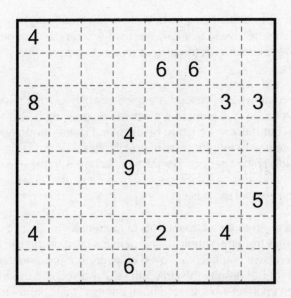

Instructions

- ☐ Draw solid lines along some of the dashed lines in order to divide the grid up into a set of rectangles, such that every number is inside exactly one rectangle.

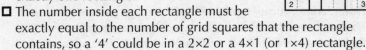

- ☐ The number inside each rectangle must be exactly equal to the number of grid squares that the rectangle contains, so a '4' could be in a 2×2 or a 4×1 (or 1×4) rectangle.
- ☐ All grid squares are used.

Re-Thinking
PERFECTION

It's a job interview cliché. "Do you have any flaws?" "Well, I can be too much of a perfectionist".

For some people this may just be a cheesy line that suggests (probably ineffectively) that they are hard-workers, but for others a struggle for perfection is too often a reason to never achieve their real goals.

Usually in life what is needed is a good-enough, but not necessarily perfect, solution. You want to get where you're going reasonably quickly – but it doesn't need to be the literal fastest route. And often there are an infinite array of possibilities where it is simply not possible to be "perfect" because perfection is in the eye of the beholder, and aiming solely for your own particular viewpoint of perfection is arbitrary at best.

The lie is given to perfection in lots of modern technology. Success often comes from the simplest, and perhaps most restrictive, designs. How often have you been annoyed by your phone, computer or microwave? But despite this they still sell, and you still use them. They aren't perfect – but they're good enough; maybe only barely so, but do you think the person who sold it to you cares?

Instructions

☐ Think about a recent occasion where your fears of not being "good enough" held you back. It could be anything: speaking at a friend's event; dressing for an evening occasion; writing an email to someone you respect; or something to do with your work.

☐ Don't judge yourself too harshly. Remember you are likely to be your own strongest critic. Other people are mostly absorbed in their own personal issues and pay only peripheral attention to those around them for most of the time.

Day 1

Day 2

EASY
PEAS
PIGEON
MONKEY

Day 3

100	97	96	95	88	87	86	85	84	83
99	98	93	94	89	76	77	78	79	82
2	3	92	91	90	75	74	73	80	81
1	4	5	42	43	50	51	72	71	70
8	7	6	41	44	49	52	57	58	69
9	14	15	40	45	48	53	56	59	68
10	13	16	39	46	47	54	55	60	67
11	12	17	38	35	34	33	32	61	66
20	19	18	37	36	27	28	31	62	65
21	22	23	24	25	26	29	30	63	64

Week 3 Solutions

Day 4

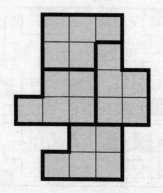

Day 5

Decode each of these quotations by replacing A with H, B with I, C with J and so on through to replacing Y with F and Z with G

Look before you leap

A bird in the hand is worth two in the bush

Day 6

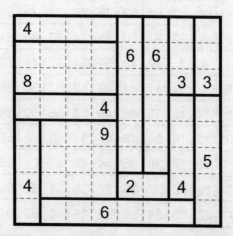

Week 4

Total Brain Points Available: **145**

Reasoning
NUMBER LINK

This route-finding puzzle requires a mix of reasoning and observation skills.

1	**2**						
		3				**3**	
4		**5**		**6**		**2**	
			7				
	4				**8**		
	7	**1**			**6**		
	5					**8**	

Instructions

- ☐ Draw a series of separate paths, each connecting a pair of identical numbers, as in the example.
- ☐ No more than one line can pass through any square, and lines can only travel horizontally or vertically between squares.

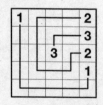

Language
ANAGRAMS

Find an anagram of the CAPITALIZED word in each sentence that can go in the gap.

1. We SPEAK of mountain _____.

2. The water TANKS _____!

3. The howl of the WOLVES seemed to consist solely of _____.

4. The man's SNORES disturbed the security _____.

5. The landlord vowed to be _____ with his RENTERS.

6. They ate _____ on board the CRUISER.

Concentration
BINARY PUZZLE

Fill the empty grid squares with 0s and 1s to make a series of binary numbers.

				1			1
		1		1			
1		1			1		
			1	0		1	0
1	0						1
	0					0	
		0	0				0
				0		0	

Instructions

☐ Place a 0 or 1 in every empty square so that there are four of each in every row and column.

☐ Reading across or down a row or column, there may be no more than two of the same digit in succession. This means that you could for example have 10011001, but 1**000**1101 would not be allowed due to the three 0s in succession.

Sudoku
SUDOKU 6×6

Try this small version of the classic number placement puzzle.

		5			
			6	1	
	3				2
4				3	
	1	2			
			1		

Instructions

☐ Place 1 to 6 exactly once each in every row, column and bold-lined 3×2 box.

Speed
LETTER ORBITS

How many English words can you find? There are about 30 in total.

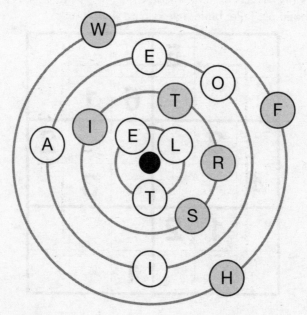

Instructions

☐ By picking one letter from the outermost orbit, then one letter from each orbit in turn through to the innermost orbit, how many four-letter English words can you find?

☐ The letters must remain in the order of the orbits, with the outermost orbit's letter first and so on.

☐ Time yourself. How many words can you find in three minutes?

Reasoning
SKYSCRAPER

In this puzzle a number inside the grid represents a skyscraper of that many floors. So a '3' is a three-storey building, while a '5' is a five-storey building. Taller buildings obscure shorter ones.

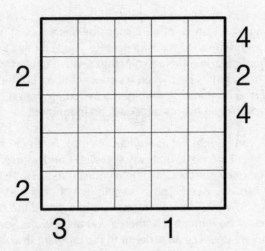

Instructions

☐ Place 1 to 5 once each into every row and column of the grid.

☐ Place buildings in the grid in such a way that each given clue number *outside* the grid represents the number of buildings that can be seen from that point, looking only at that clue's row or column.

☐ A building with a higher value always obscures a building with a lower value, while a building with a lower value never obscures a building with a higher value.

Re-Thinking
FOCUS

Have you tried solving the puzzles in this book while simultaneously having a conversation? Maybe you can do that more or less okay, but you'd be sure to slow down if you tried two puzzles at the same time. And so it is in life in general.

Many of us are incapable of escaping all distractions, whether that's work colleagues, family or other responsibilities we can't put off, but if you can find time to set aside just for yourself this can be important, particularly if there's something you're really trying to get done. Your brain works best when it's concentrating on things, and, for those of us who find a certain inertia in getting started on some tasks, distractions can even lead to task abandonment.

Distractions can be internal as well as external. Try to finish one task before you begin the next. That way you won't find yourself thinking about both at once, and you will help yourself relax by "letting go" of the one you've finished. This is something your brain really does do – think of how you instantly forget you had a cold the day after it's gone, no matter how much it bothered you at the time. Some waiters remember every detail of an order until the moment the bill is paid, at which point they forget them almost instantaneously. Your brain is pretty remarkable at organizing things, if you let it!

Instructions

- ☐ Tell someone the task you're going to do next and when you'll have it done by. Vocalizing what you're going to do can really help.
- ☐ When brain training with this book, try to focus on doing just the puzzle you're working on. Try to finish it before you move onto the next one.
- ☐ Set aside 5-10 minutes a day, if you can, to work on this book.

Score　　　Total Brain Points

Week 4 Solutions

Day 1

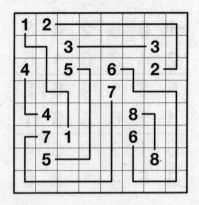

Day 2

PEAKS
STANK
VOWELS
SENSOR
STERNER
CURRIES

Day 3

0	1	0	0	1	0	1	1
0	0	1	0	1	0	1	1
1	0	1	1	0	1	0	0
0	1	0	1	0	1	1	0
1	0	1	0	1	0	0	1
0	0	1	1	0	1	0	1
1	1	0	0	1	0	1	0
1	1	0	1	0	1	0	0

Week 4 Solutions

Day 4

1	6	5	2	4	3
2	4	3	6	1	5
5	3	1	4	6	2
4	2	6	5	3	1
6	1	2	3	5	4
3	5	4	1	2	6

Day 5

Possible words include:
FAIL, FARE, FAST, FATE, FETE, FIRE, FIST, FOIL,
FORE, FORT, HAIL, HARE, HART, HAST, HATE, HERE,
HIRE, HOSE, HOST, WAIL, WAIT, WARE, WART, WATT,
WERE, WERT, WEST, WIRE, WISE, WORE, WORT

Day 6

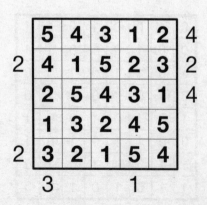

Week 5

Total Brain Points Available: **145**

Reasoning
SLITHERLINK

Just draw a loop, in this incredibly pure logic puzzle.

```
 .   .   .   .   .   .   .   .   .
   2   2       1       2
 .   .   .   .   .   .   .   .   .
 3       2       2       2
 .   .   .   .   .   .   .   .   .
 3       2       1   3       3
 .   .   .   .   .   .   .   .   .
 2       3                   3
 .   .   .   .   .   .   .   .   .
 3                   2       3
 .   .   .   .   .   .   .   .   .
 3       3   3       3       3
 .   .   .   .   .   .   .   .   .
     1       2       2       2
 .   .   .   .   .   .   .   .   .
     2       3       3   3
 .   .   .   .   .   .   .   .   .
```

Instructions

- Draw a single loop by connecting together the dots so that each numbered square has the specified number of adjacent line segments.
- Dots can only be joined by straight horizontal or vertical lines.
- The loop cannot touch, cross or overlap itself in any way.

Language

CODEWORD

Work out the number-to-letter substitution code to create a regular filled crossword grid, which uses only standard English words.

		6	23	10	18		18	7	4	19		
A												**N**
B	4 **R**		5		1	24	6 **E**		10		15	**O**
C	6	21	7	15	5		5	10	8	6	2	**P**
D	14		17		2		5		6		2	**Q**
E	6	11	6	2		12	15	18	16	1	4	**R**
F												**S**
G	17				14		4				6	**T**
H	19	6	18	1	17	6		15	14	9	14	**U**
I	5		1		6		15		24		14	**V**
J												**W**
K	6	13	18	6	5		25	7	10	18	6	**X**
L	14		1		5	6	15		22		14	**Y**
M		3	15	20 **Z**	11		4	10	26	14		**Z**

1	2	3	4	5	6	7	8	9	10	11	12	13
14	15	16	17	18	19	20	21	22	23	24	25	26

Number Skills

NUMBER DARTS

Can you hit the given totals on this number dartboard?

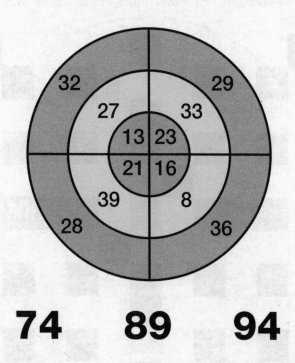

Instructions

☐ By choosing exactly one number from each ring of this dartboard, can you find three numbers whose values add up to the first listed total? Now repeat with the other two totals.

☐ For example, you could form 61 with 32 + 8 + 21.

Score   Total Brain Points

Observation
SUBDIVISION

This puzzle will test your spatial reasoning.

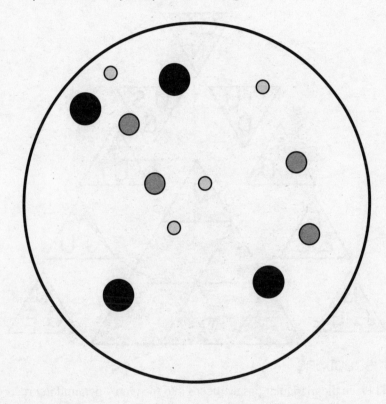

Instructions

☐ Draw two straight lines in order to divide this circle up into exactly four areas.
☐ Each area must contain one of each size of shaded circle.
☐ The lines you draw should start at one edge of the outer shape and cross all the way to another edge of the outer shape.

Language

LETTER TRIANGLES

Can you fit all the letter jigsaw pieces to spell out one word per row?

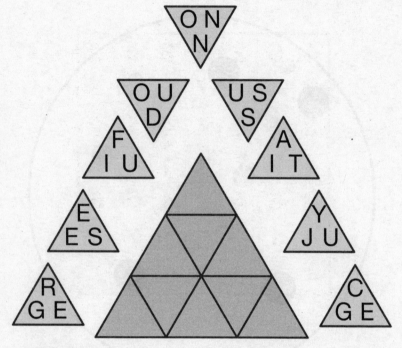

Instructions

☐ Place the triangular jigsaw pieces into the empty pyramid in order to spell out a word reading across each row. There are therefore six words to be found.

☐ Each piece is used only once and may not be rotated or reflected – place them in exactly the same orientation as they are given.

Reasoning
HITORI

This puzzle is in some respects like Sudoku in reverse!

4	5	2	6	3	4	2
7	4	1	7	2	3	6
3	6	2	7	4	1	2
4	2	7	1	1	4	5
2	6	4	3	4	5	6
4	1	6	5	1	7	4
4	3	3	2	6	3	7

Instructions

- ☐ Shade in squares so that no number occurs more than once per row or column.
- ☐ Shaded squares cannot touch in either a horizontal or vertical direction.
- ☐ All unshaded squares must form a single continuous area, so you can move left/right/up/down from one unshaded square to another to reach any unshaded square.

2	7	8	8	6	8	3	3
5	1	6	1	2	3	4	2
7	6	2	8	5	4	8	3
3	2	4	5	4	7	6	8
8	5	5	8	7	4	2	3
3	8	3	4	2	5	7	1
4	5	3	7	8	2	1	3
1	3	1	2	1	6	7	4

Re-Thinking
DEADLINES

"It will be finished... soon."

You could probably think of countless things you started but never finished, or intended to do but never did. Whether at the individual level or on a much larger level (think of the government projects that over-run or never deliver), lack of discipline is often the reason for a whole range of things that perhaps should be called failures.

Sometimes these don't matter, but all too often they do. When there is something important to be done, set yourself a deadline. And don't just say "well, I think I'll have it done by next week". Be strict with yourself. Set a deadline. Write it down. Stick it up on the wall. Highlight it. Look at it every day and see if you're on track. Tell someone you're going to stick to it and make them promise to bug you if you don't.

One of the key reasons people fail at life improvement tasks such as dieting is that they put things off until some mythical "tomorrow", by saying that they'll start them the next day. But then when it comes to tomorrow, well, it's only one more day until the next "tomorrow"...

Make tomorrow today. Set a deadline, and start while you still have time to hit it – or beat it!

Instructions

☐ Look at your task list you wrote at the end of week two. Have you started any of them? Are your deadlines still realistic?

☐ Be disciplined. Find something to look forward to and set it aside as a reward for yourself which you get only when the task is completed. If you can get someone else to oversee this to help enforce that discipline then even better!

Week 5 Solutions

Day 1

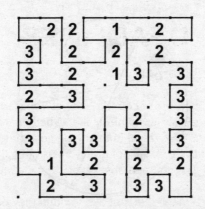

Day 2

Day 3

$$74 = 28 + 33 + 13$$

$$89 = 29 + 39 + 21$$

$$94 = 32 + 39 + 23$$

Day 4

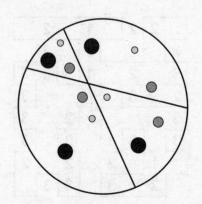

Day 5

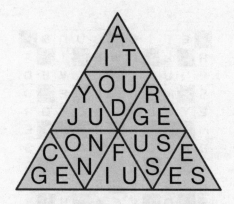

Day 6

4	5	2	6	3	4	2
7	4	1	7	2	3	6
3	6	2	7	4	1	2
4	2	7	1	1	4	5
2	6	4	3	4	5	6
4	1	6	5	1	7	4
4	3	3	2	6	3	7

Week 6

Total Brain Points Available: **140**

Reasoning
HANJIE

This popular picture-revealing puzzle is published under a range of names, including Griddler™, Nonogram and Pic-a-pix.

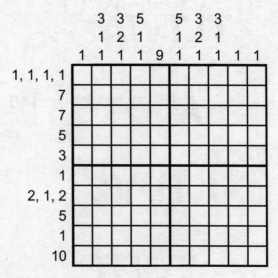

Picture clue: Spring time decoration

Instructions

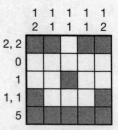

- ☐ Shade in squares in the grid to reveal a picture by obeying the clue constraints at the start of each row or column.
- ☐ The clues provide, in order, the length of every run of consecutive shaded squares in their row or column.
- ☐ There must be a gap of at least one empty square between each run of shaded squares in the same row or column.

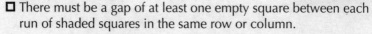

Language
WORD SEQUENCES

Can you work out the famous novel titles represented by these initials? Each of these books has sold over 50 million copies.

TLTWATW

ATOTC

TDVC

TCITR

HPATDH

TEHL

Concentration
KING'S JOURNEY

Fill the grid squares to reveal a hidden path, which can include diagonal moves.

	41	40	46		5	
			64	51			
				8	2	
	62	53		1		10
36		58	56	54		12	
35				26		
33	34	30				
		22		17		

Instructions

☐ Fill empty squares so that the completed grid contains every number from 1 to 64 exactly once each.

☐ Place the numbers so that there is a route from 1 to 64 that visits every grid square exactly once each in numerical order, moving only left, right, up, down or diagonally between touching squares.

Observation
CIRCUIT BOARD

Which piece fits in the gap?

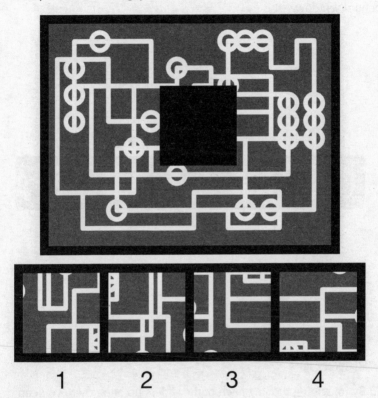

1   2   3   4

Instructions

☐ Can you work out which one of the four pieces fits into the gap, in order to complete the circuit board? Once complete all of the lines will connect at both ends.

☐ You may need to rotate the correct piece.

Speed

WORD SLIDER

Imagine you've cut out each of these columns of letters, plus the central window.

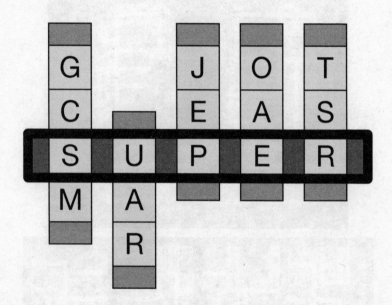

Instructions

☐ By imagining moving each of the sliders up and down, you can reveal different letters and read words through the central window.

☐ Each word must use a letter from every slider – you can't slide them out of the window. Therefore each word will be five letters long.

☐ One word is spelled out for you already. Can you find six further English words in just 90 seconds?

Total Brain Points

Reasoning
ARROWS

One of the keys to being able to solve this puzzle is working out a good way of making notes, so you can keep track of your deductions.

2	0	3
4	1	4
6	4	4

Instructions

☐ Place an arrow into every box outside the grid. Each arrow can point up, down, left, right or in one of the four principle diagonal directions.

☐ Every arrow must point to at least one number.

☐ When correctly placed, the numbers in the grid must be equal to the count of the number of arrows that are pointing at that number.

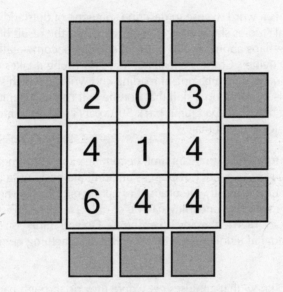

Re-Thinking

THE GENESIS OF GENIUS

Einstein was a genius, or so most people would agree. But was he born that way, or did he become that thanks to his own efforts?

"Genius" is a word we use to describe someone of outstanding ability, but studies show that genius is really just the result of a lot of effort – perhaps about 10,000 hours of effort to become really good at most activities. Crudely-speaking, that's how long it takes us as we grow up to become amazing at reading and writing, which sadly for our egos is so common a skill that no one will call us a genius for mastering them. And yet jump back 500 years and you might have been heralded as just that.

It's easier to spend significant time becoming expert at something when you start as a kid, but even as an adult the basic principle holds. Genius is mostly the product of hard work. Those who are incredibly skilled at one thing can be of only average skill – or even far below average – at many other things. Do you think you'd beat Rafael Nadal at tennis? Definitely not. But at something else? Quite possibly.

It helps to know that geniuses get where they do through hard work. It means there's no intrinsic reason why you can't excel, too.

Instructions

☐ Is there something you want to be better at? Then start practising it. You have nothing to lose, and you will certainly become better at it. It's the only sure way to improve.

☐ You can practise physical activities in your head, without actually doing them. Studies have shown this really works – your brain can learn what to do by just thinking about tensing the right muscles.

☐ You are much smarter and more capable than you think. If other people are better, perhaps they have merely practised more.

Score   Total Brain Points

Week 6 Solutions

Day 1

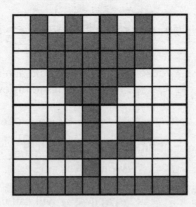

Day 2

The Lion, The Witch and the Wardrobe
A Tale of Two Cities
The Da Vinci Code
The Catcher in the Rye
Harry Potter and the Deathly Hallows
The Eagle Has Landed

Day 3

42	41	40	46	47	48	5	6
43	39	45	64	51	49	7	4
38	44	63	52	50	8	2	3
37	61	62	53	55	1	9	10
36	60	58	56	54	27	12	11
35	59	57	29	28	26	19	13
33	34	30	24	25	20	18	14
32	31	23	22	21	17	16	15

Week 6 Solutions

Day 4

Circuit piece 4

Day 5

Possible words include:
CAPER
CAPES
GAPES
GREAT
GREET
MAJOR
SUPER (already given)

Day 6

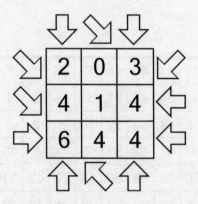

Week 7

Total Brain Points Available: **125**

Reasoning
EASY AS ABC

Place A, B and C in every row and column, using the external clues.

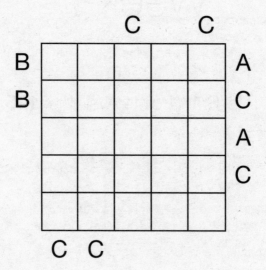

Instructions

☐ Fit the letters A, B and C exactly once each into every row and column of squares inside the empty grid. Two squares in each row or column will therefore be empty.

☐ Letters outside the grid indicate which letter appears closest to that end of the row or column.

Language
COMPREHENSION

Read the following series of statements, then fill out the empty table at the bottom of the page appropriately.

Three different occasions are being celebrated with presents. Each present is wrapped in a different colour paper, using a different type of decoration. Can you work out which of each of the following go together? Write your conclusion in the table below.

Colours: Red, Gold, Silver
Decorations: Bow, Ribbon, Glitter
Occasions: Birthday, Christmas, Romance

1. The present wrapped in the ribbon did not use the silver wrapping paper.

2. Christmas was not the occasion on which the gold-wrapped present was given.

3. The romantic present was decorated with glitter.

4. The bow was stuck on to the outside of the present wrapped in red.

Colour	Decoration	Occasion

Number Skills
NUMBER PYRAMID

Complete this number pyramid using just addition and subtraction.

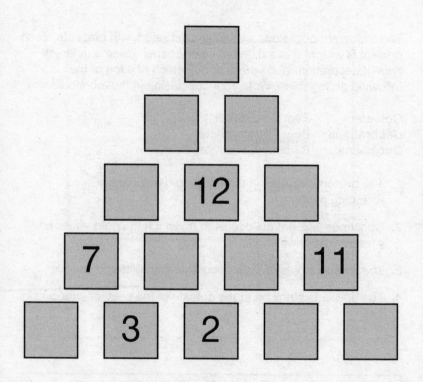

Instructions

☐ Fill in empty bricks so that each brick contains a value equal to the sum of the two bricks directly beneath it.

Score   Total Brain Points

Sudoku
JIGSAW 6×6

This slight twist on Sudoku ramps up the difficulty level more than you might expect!

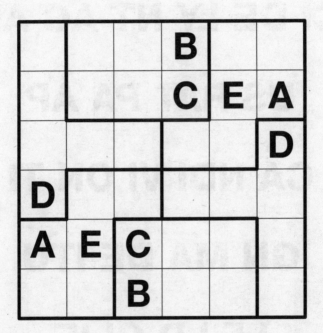

Instructions

☐ Place 1 to 6 once each into every row, column and bold-lined jigsaw region.

Language
WORD FRAGMENTS

Rearrange the fragments on each line to make a complete word.

CI DE LY NT AC AL

US RAT PA AP

CA NDI VI ON TI

GN MA DE ITU

LF LD OI IE

SM AS ES CL AT

Reasoning

NURIKABE

This Japanese logic puzzle is sometimes called Islands in the Stream.

			5					
							8	
								4
3				4				
			1					4
5								
	8							
					2			

Instructions

☐ Shade in squares so that every number in the puzzle remains as part of a continuous unshaded area of precisely the given number of squares.

☐ There can be only one number per unshaded area.

☐ Shaded squares cannot form any solid 2×2 (or larger) areas.

☐ All the shaded squares must form one continuous area.

Re-Thinking
STRESS

Most of us feel some stress from time to time, and that in itself is not necessarily a problem. A little bit of stress can be a great motivator to get things done, or to help us focus on what's important. It's a biological response that makes us concentrate.

Too much stress, however, can be debilitating. Like freezing in the path of a car on a busy road, it's not a useful biological response in the modern world. So if stress is ruining your life, you absolutely must try to do something about it. It may be easy to say, and some of us have stressful things in our lives that in practice we can't avoid, but even if you can't avoid the sources of the stress then you can almost certainly still do something to help alleviate them.

Laughter is amazing. It relaxes you, easing stress. So is exercise – go for a walk, or join a gym (or if you're a member then actually go). You may have a hundred reasons why you are putting it off, but forget them and try it. And if you feel better afterwards (which you will) then remember that feeling and not all the reasons for inertia.

Social contact is the most natural thing for your brain. We are social animals, biologically-speaking, and convivial social contact will literally help you feel better. Make sure you find time to relax.

Instructions

- ☐ Laugh. Watch some comedy on TV, read a funny book, buy a child's book of appalling jokes; whatever it is, laugh. Out loud, if you can!
- ☐ Some people use alcohol or other stimulants to help relax, but these don't help in the long term. Learn to relax without them. Laughter in a social setting brings on all the same positive symptoms as light drinking, but is both cheaper and better for you.
- ☐ Take deep breaths. Go ahead – it works! It releases tension.

Week 7 Solutions

Day 1

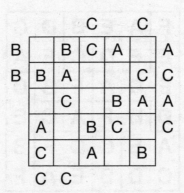

Day 2

Gold - Ribbon - Birthday
Silver - Glitter - Romance
Red - Bow - Christmas

Day 3

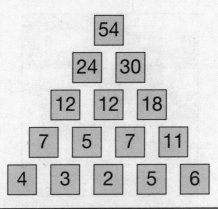

Week 7 Solutions

Day 4

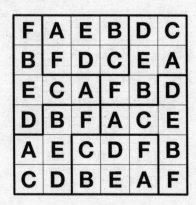

F	A	E	B	D	C
B	F	D	C	E	A
E	C	A	F	B	D
D	B	F	A	C	E
A	E	C	D	F	B
C	D	B	E	A	F

Day 5

ACCIDENTALLY
APPARATUS
VINDICATION
MAGNITUDE
OILFIELD
CLASSMATES

Day 6

Week 8

Total Brain Points Available: **220**

Reasoning

HASHI

The full Japanese name of this puzzle is Hashiwokakero, but it is often also known as Bridges.

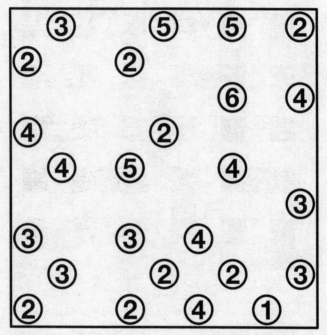

Instructions

☐ Join circled numbers with horizontal or vertical lines.

☐ Each number must have as many lines connected to it as specified by its value.

☐ No more than two lines may join any pair of numbers.

☐ No lines may cross.

☐ The finished layout must allow you to travel from any number to any other number just by following one or more lines.

Language
CRYPTIC CROSSWORD

Each clue contains both a straight and a cryptic definition.

Across

1 Western lost nothing for a passing note (10)

7 Nothing penned without a name was released (6)

8 Multiple identities go in two directions (4)

9 National condition (5)

11 Second note stirred a gem (5)

13 Get the French into the vehicle - understood? (5)

14 Dead prince came back - and possibly rose? (5)

16 Retired leading duo sent outsiders for break (4)

18 One of two, I wandered in the clear air (6)

20 Deals with a good quantity of paper, swapping notes on leisure activities (10)

Down

2 I, for example, trump it most of all (7)

3 Particle takes Roubles out of metal (3)

4 Dispatch all about objectives (4)

5 Letters arranged on board table (7)

6 Left, having nothing again at card game (3)

10 Pulls cart back to hill? (7)

12 Closest Eastern development? (7)

15 Simple me, with reference (4)

17 Some generation? (3)

19 Time apart from money is a bind (3)

Number Skills
NUMBER SEQUENCES

Using your mathematical skills, can you work out what comes next in each sequence?

3, 7, 11, 15, 19, ?

4, 8, 16, 32, 64, ?

43, 47, 53, 59, 61, ?

191, 172, 154, 137, 121, ?

51, 53, 57, 65, 81, ?

Reasoning
KAKURO

This Japanese number crossword is also called Cross Sums.

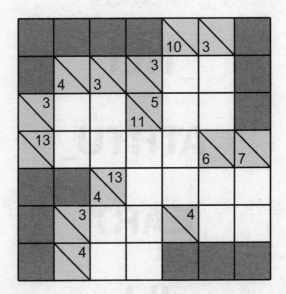

Instructions

☐ Place a digit from 1 to 9 into each white square to solve the clues.

☐ Each horizontal run of white squares adds up to the total above the diagonal line to the left of the run, and each vertical run of white squares adds up to the total below the diagonal line above the run.

☐ No digit can be used more than once in any run.

Language
START AND END

For each line, can you find the missing letter that can be added to both the start and end to make a normal English word? For example, N could be added to _OO_ to make NOON.

TILT

ATHTU

EART

ILL

ULLAR

HAKE

Reasoning
CORRAL

This logic puzzle involves building a fence around the given clues.

			3	2			2
	7						
	6					9	
	7	3				10	4
5	6				8	12	
	6					9	
						9	
5			6	5			

Instructions

☐ Draw a single loop along the grid lines such that each clue number can 'see' the given number of squares within the loop.

☐ The number of squares that a clue can see is the total count of interior squares in both horizontal and vertical directions from that square, including the clue square itself (which is only counted once).

☐ The loop cannot cross or touch itself, even at a corner.

Re-Thinking
MEMORY TRAINING

Challenge your brain each day with new activities. This book is a great start, but there are some areas it doesn't cover directly, such as explicit memory training – although many of the puzzles will develop short-term memory skills anyway, as you hold deductions in your head or remember sudoku digits that you've placed.

When it comes to the direct recall of facts, you have short-term and long-term memory. The former will help you remember a telephone number or email address 10 seconds later, while the latter helps you recall information days, or even years, after you last saw it.

Many techniques exist for improving your long-term memory, and your brain will adapt over time as you expand your knowledge, but it's your short-term memory that will respond most directly to brain training exercises. Improvements in short-term memory can be achieved just by practising using it, and what's more they've been shown to last many years even after you stop explicitly training.

It's a good idea to invent small memory exercises for yourself. They can be really simple – for example try reading the first paragraph at the top of this page, then turn the page and see if you can write out the exact sentence, complete with punctuation. Challenge your short-term memory whenever you can.

Instructions

☐ Write an eight-digit number on a piece of paper, then turn it over. Wait a few seconds, then try to write out the number on another sheet. If that's too easy, change to a nine-digit number, and then keep using longer numbers until you are sufficiently challenged.

☐ If you find that task too easy, write down a series of separate numbers (for example 24, 75, 93, 254, 12) and try memorising those, extending the activity as you need to keep the challenge up.

Week 8 Solutions

Day 1

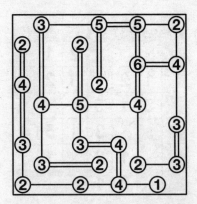

Day 2

Day 3

23: Add 4 at each step
128: Multiply by 2 at each step
67: Prime numbers in increasing order
106: Difference one less at each step
113: Difference doubles at each step

Week 8 Solutions

Day 4

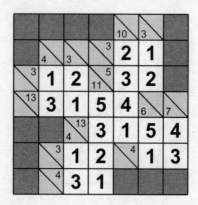

Day 5

STILTS
BATHTUB
HEARTH
SILLS
DULLARD
SHAKES

Day 6

			3	2			2
	7						
	6					9	
	7	3				10	4
5	6				8	12	
	6					9	
						9	
5			6	5			

Week 9

Total Brain Points Available: **145**

Reasoning
DIAGONAL NUMBER LINK

This puzzle is considerably harder than regular Number Link!

1					2
		2			3
4				5	6
			6		
5	1		7		
7				4	3

Instructions

☐ Draw a series of separate paths, each connecting a pair of identical numbers, as in the example.

☐ No more than one line can pass through any square. They can only cross if they do so diagonally on the join between four squares.

☐ Lines can travel horizontally, vertically or diagonally between squares.

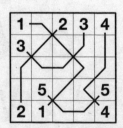

Language
LETTER SOUP

Rearrange these floating letters to spell out the names of five single-word Winter Olympics sports. Each letter will be used in exactly one word.

Reasoning
LIGHTHOUSES

Can you locate all the ships in a stormy sea?

3		**1**		**3**		**1**			
3									
						1			
		2							
						1			
		0							
								3	
		1		**0**		**1**		**0**	

Instructions

☐ Black squares with numbers on represent lighthouses. The number reveals how many ships can see that lighthouse. Ships can see a lighthouse if they are in the same row or column as the lighthouse.

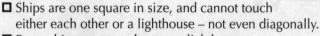

☐ Ships are one square in size, and cannot touch either each other or a lighthouse – not even diagonally.

☐ Every ship can see at least one lighthouse.

Observation
MAZE

Find a path from the lighter circle (at the top) to the darker circle.

Language
LINK WORDS

Find a common English word to place in each gap, so that when attached to the end of the previous word or the start of the following word this makes two more English words. For example, BIRTH and BREAK could be linked with DAY, making BIRTHDAY and DAYBREAK.

MIT ___ DON

FURTHER ___ OVER

OUT ___ BACK

There are three possible solutions for this final pair of words.

Reasoning
LINESWEEPER

This Minesweeper variant uses lines instead of mines!

	3						
			7		7		
5			5				
						6	
	7					8	
			5				

Instructions

☐ Draw a single loop made up of horizontal and vertical lines.

☐ The loop can't cross or touch itself, and can only pass through empty grid squares.

☐ Squares with numbers indicate how many touching squares the loop passes through, including diagonally-touching squares.

Re-Thinking

NUMBERS EVERYWHERE

There are numbers all around you, from store prices to recipe quantities to arrival times and so on. They're part of the fabric of our lives, and yet there are some of us who just don't like them. In fact, some people convince themselves that they "can't do numbers". Of course that isn't really true – everyone can "do numbers" reasonably well if they choose to; we have innate abilities, and at the very least anyone can count to 10 using their fingers and thumbs!

If you look at a small group of objects you can guess fairly accurately how many there are. You can try dropping random clutches of cards, or stones, or dice, or tomatoes, or whatever you have handy. How many do you think you dropped? You're probably pretty close. You can estimate just fine, if you choose to. These skills apply equally well to making sure a store assistant isn't either incompetent or crooked. The secret is in the guessing – your natural estimating skills.

When you were at school, chances are that mathematics was about precision, and being exactly right. But in real life you just need to be close. Work out roughly how much you expect to spend; don't count every penny, but round numbers and make a guess. Any guess is better than no guess! If a checkout total isn't near your guess, check it more slowly – use the calculator on your phone if you need to!

Instructions

☐ You are very good at realizing when something's wrong – it can feel like a sixth sense, but really it's just your brain telling you things without you being consciously aware of what it's working out. This ability applies to number skills too, so don't shut down your natural talents – use them!

☐ Add up your shopping as you go, or even just look at your basket and estimate with a glance. Have an idea what the total cost will be. Make complex numbers simple by discarding the pennies.

Week 9 Solutions

Day 1

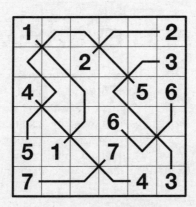

Day 2

CURLING

LUGE

BOBSLEIGH

SKELETON

SNOWBOARD

Day 3

Week 9 Solutions

Day 4

Day 5

TEN: MITTEN and TENDON

MORE: FURTHERMORE and MOREOVER

COME: OUTCOME and COMEBACK
or SET: OUTSET and SETBACK
or: PLAY: OUTPLAY and PLAYBACK

Day 6

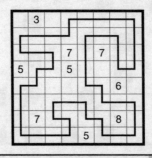

Week 10

Total Brain Points Available: **180**

Reasoning
TREN

This Japanese puzzle requires you to place blocks into a grid.

	1		0		
	1	0			
			1		2
1					

Instructions

□ Draw 1x2 and 1x3 rectangular blocks along the grid lines such that each number is contained in exactly one block.

□ The number in each block reveals the total count of squares the block can slide into. Vertical blocks slide in their columns; horizontal blocks slide in their rows.

□ In the example, the '2' in the top row can slide up/down into two squares; the bottom row '1' can slide left/right into one square.

Language
NEXT IN SEQUENCE

Can you work out what letter should come next in these two sequences? The sequences may be either initials or some other sequence of single letter identifiers.

For example, M T W T F would be followed by S, for Monday, Tuesday, Wednesday, Thursday, Friday and then Saturday.

O T T F F

I V X L C

Number Skills
FLOATING NUMBERS

For an extra challenge, try solving this entirely in your head!

17   **30**

20   **28**

13   **11**

24

Instructions

☐ Can you work out which of the floating numbers above you can add together to make each of the following totals?

☐ You can't use a floating number more than once in any given total.

60   **88**   **110**

Observation

REARRANGEMENT

This puzzle is a great test of your visual imagination skills.

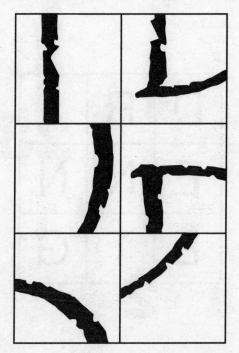

Instructions

- ☐ Using just your imagination, work out which letter you would be able to form if you were to cut out and rearrange the positions of these six tiles.
- ☐ You can't rotate (or flip over/mirror image) any of the pieces – just imagine sliding them to new positions.

Speed
WORD SQUARE

How many words can you find in this square?

There are at least 25 to be found.

Instructions

- ☐ Make a word by starting on any letter and then tracing a path to adjacent letters, moving only to touching squares (including diagonally-touching squares).
- ☐ Every word must be at least three letters in length.
- ☐ The path can cross itself but it can't use any letter square more than once in a given word.
- ☐ There is a word that uses every square. Can you find it?
- ☐ Time yourself. How many words can you find in three minutes?

Reasoning
KROPKI

This puzzle combines a Latin Square with additional clues.

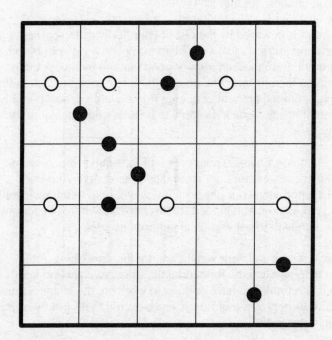

Instructions

☐ Place 1 to 5 once each into every row and column.

☐ Two squares with a black dot between contain numbers where one is twice the value of the other.

☐ Two squares with a white dot between contain consecutive numbers, such as 2 and 3, or 5 and 6.

☐ All possible black/white dots are given. If there is no dot, adjacent numbers are neither consecutive nor twice/half each other.

☐ Between 1 and 2 *either* a white or a black dot can be given.

Re-Thinking

PHYSICAL FITNESS

You might feel that your intelligence and your physical fitness are separate entities, but that isn't true.

Your brain is powered by the rest of your body, and in particular the oxygen and nutrients that your heart pumps to it via your blood. If that pumping isn't fast enough or good enough then your brain will suffer; you literally won't be able to think fast enough. Each brain cell has a limited amount of energy stored within it, so when it is used up it needs a quick resupply to be able to fire again for the next thought.

Your brain consumes 20 per cent of all the energy you consume, despite accounting for only around two per cent of your body weight. Improving your physical fitness will help to improve your blood circulation, and indeed studies have shown that better physical fitness can lead to better mental performance.

Physical fitness and your weight are not the same thing – it is perfectly possible to be thin and unfit, or overweight and fairly fit. So even if you think you have nothing to work on, the chances are you can always improve your fitness level, even if that's just by walking a few minutes further a day.

Instructions

☐ Particularly if you work at a desk, make sure you take regular breaks during the day and that you move around when you can.
☐ Find time to walk or do whatever physical exercise is appropriate for your current fitness level. Most of us have a good idea what that is, but don't be afraid to ask an expert if you need to. Not just the rest of your body, but your brain also will thank you for it – you really can exercise yourself smarter!
☐ Try working after exercising – do you find you feel more alert?

Total Brain Points

Week 10 Solutions

Day 1

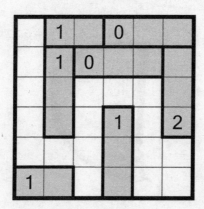

Day 2

S
Numbers in increasing value:
One Two Three Four Five Six

D
Roman Numerals in increasing value:
I (=1) V (=5) X (=10) L (=50) C (=100) D (=500)

Day 3

$$60 = 13 + 17 + 30$$

$$88 = 13 + 17 + 28 + 30$$

$$110 = 11 + 17 + 24 + 28 + 30$$

Week 10 Solutions

Day 4

Day 5

Possible words include:
DEE, DEN, DENT, END, ENTER, ENTERING, INN, INNER, INTEND, INTER, INTERN, IRE, NEE, NEED, NERD, NET, NINE, RED, REND, RENT, RIND, RING, TEE, TEED, TEEN, TEN, TEND, TENDER, TENDERING, TERN

Day 6

3	5	2	4	1
2	4	1	3	5
5	2	4	1	3
4	1	3	5	2
1	3	5	2	4

Week 11

Total Brain Points Available: **175**

Reasoning
MASYU

This puzzle involves finding a loop through all of the circles.

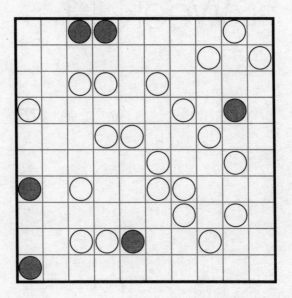

Instructions

- ☐ Draw a single loop that passes through the centre of every circle. Diagonal lines are not allowed.
- ☐ On a shaded circle the loop must turn 90 degrees and continue straight for at least one square on either side of the shaded circle.
- ☐ On a white circle the loop cannot turn, but it must then turn 90 degrees on either one or both of the adjacent squares.
- ☐ The loop cannot enter any square more than once.

Language

WORD CHAINS

Can you travel from the top to the bottom of these word chains?

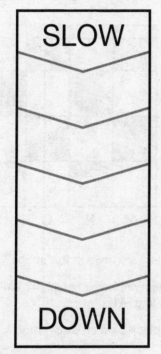

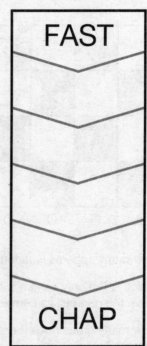

Instructions

- ☐ Fill in the empty steps with normal English words.
- ☐ At each step down the chain change just one letter to make a new word, but don't rearrange the other letters.
- ☐ There may be multiple ways to solve each chain, but you only need to find one solution per chain.

Observation
IMAGE COMBINATION

How good are you at combining images in your head?

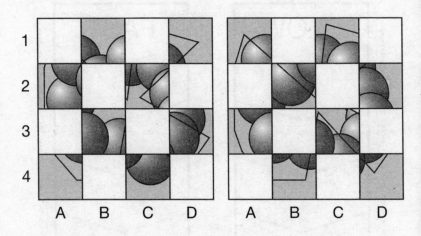

1. How many spheres (shaded circles) are there in this image?

2. Which is the only sphere without any spheres behind it? Write down the grid cell its centre is in (e.g. A1).

3. How many times does the solid black path cross over the spheres?

Instructions

- ☐ Imagine overlaying the two images above, so the gaps in one are filled with the content from the other.
- ☐ Answer the written questions, based on the combined image.

Sudoku

KILLER SUDOKU 6×6

This Sudoku variant requires some simple adding up to solve.

Instructions

- ☐ Place 1 to 6 once each into every row, column and 3×2 box, while obeying the cage totals.
- ☐ The contents of each dashed line cage must sum to the total given at the top-left.
- ☐ You **cannot repeat a number** within a dashed line cage.

Speed
CRISS CROSS

Fit all of the listed words into the grid, crossword-style. How many can you place within just three minutes?

3 Letters
Eek
Egg
Lei
Use

5 Letters
Clips
Every

Issue
Ratio
Roads
There

6 Letters
Ascend
Eclair
Except

League
Sister
Worked

7 Letters
Genetic
Offices
Refusal
Shortly

9 Letters
Accounted
Emergence
Overrides
Preserves

11 Letters
Convenience
Personality

Reasoning
FOUR WINDS

This logic puzzle is a good test of your spatial thinking.

			8	7			
3							4
		2			2		
1							2
		3			2		
2							3
			3	3			
		2			1		

Instructions

- ☐ Draw a horizontal or vertical line in every empty square, either passing through or stopping in that square.
- ☐ Lines must start at a black square.
- ☐ Numbers on black squares indicate the total number of white squares entered by lines starting at that square.
- ☐ Lines can only run horizontally and vertically and cannot bend.
- ☐ Lines can't cross, or touch more than one black square.

Re-Thinking
KEEPING THINGS FUN

If you aren't enjoying something you will find it harder to stick to doing it, whatever it is. The same applies to almost anything, including brain training, which is for example why this book is designed to have such a wide range of puzzle types – even though there will be some you like less than others, you should regularly be coming across a type you enjoy.

The level of fun and reward in an activity can, of course, depend on the effort you put in yourself, and often it will be the case that an activity gets progressively easier as you become more skilled at it. The key to self-improvement, then, is to find the right challenge for your current level so that a task is "good for you" without being so difficult that you end up giving up entirely. It's also about not giving up before you get to the reward point – work out what the reward is and, if it's worth going for it, then keep on reminding yourself of that.

Generally, try to find the fun in an activity. If you don't enjoy the gym, take up a sport instead, or go swimming. If you don't like solving sudoku, try a crossword instead. If you don't enjoy a task, find the game in it – even if that game is something that in itself has no real purpose, it can help motivate you to keep going, and it can certainly provide the odd smile in an otherwise serious activity.

Instructions

☐ Think of an activity or task you feel you should be doing that you have been putting off or do too infrequently. The chances are this is something you haven't persisted with very much. Try again, if you can, and see if it gets more pleasant after several attempts. If it's not immediately rewarding enough for you, then work out what the rewards should be. Are they in the future? Can you measure your progress towards them? Can you find some more immediate rewards, or games to amuse you along the way?

Week 11 Solutions

Day 1

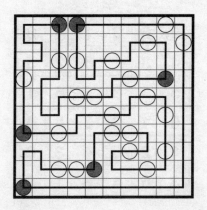

Day 2

SLOW
SLOT
SOOT
SOON
SOWN
DOWN

FAST
CAST
COST
COAT
CHAT
CHAP

Day 3

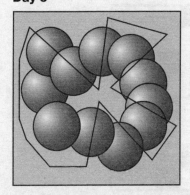

1) 11 spheres

2) A2

3) 6 times

Day 4

2	5	6	1	4	3
4	3	1	6	2	5
5	4	3	2	6	1
6	1	2	3	5	4
1	2	5	4	3	6
3	6	4	5	1	2

Day 5

Day 6

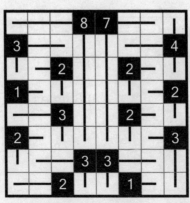

Week 12

Total Brain Points Available: **180**

Reasoning
HEYAWAKE

This Japanese logic puzzle's name translates as "Divided Rooms".

Instructions

□ Shade some squares, such that no two shaded squares are adjacent, except diagonally, and all unshaded squares form a single continuous area.

□ Any single horizontal or vertical line of unshaded squares cannot cross more than one bold line.

□ Numbered squares may or may not be shaded, but always give the precise amount of shaded squares in their bold-lined region.

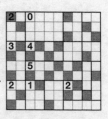

Language
MULTI-ANAGRAM

Can you find the given number of anagrams of each of the following sets of letters? Each anagram must be a standard English word, and it must use *all* of the given letters once each.

4 anagrams:

E E E R R S V

3 anagrams:

A C G I N O S T

3 anagrams:

A C E E R R S T

Reasoning
BATTLESHIPS

Find the ships in this solo version of the classic two-player game.

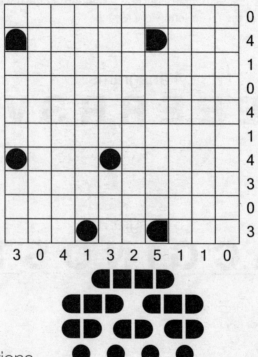

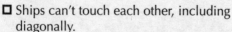

Instructions

☐ Locate the position of each of the listed ships in the grid. Ships are placed horizontally or vertically only.

☐ Numbers around the edge tell you the number of ship segments in each row and column.

☐ Ships can't touch each other, including diagonally.

☐ Some ship segments are already given.

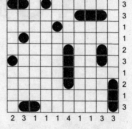

Observation

PHRASEOLOGY

This illustration represents a well-known phrase. Can you work out what it is?

This second illustration represents a well-known book. Can you work out what book that is?

GNIK EHT

Language
ARROWWORD

Solve this crossword where the clues are written inside the grid.

Christmas animal	▼	Slippery fish	▼	Indigenous inhabitants	▼	SMS 'Oh, also' (inits)
Incident ▶				▼		Required
Lodge		Mown grass ▶				▼
▶			Depressions		No more than	
Dearest		Green citrus fruit ▶	▼		▼	
▶						
Intersected		Lived ▶				
▶						

Reasoning
TOROIDAL NUMBER LINK

This puzzle allows lines to 'wrap around' from one side of the puzzle to the other!

1			2	3
4				
	5		3	
				4
5	2			1

Instructions

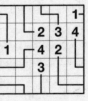

- ☐ Draw a series of separate paths, each connecting a pair of identical numbers, as in the example.
- ☐ No more than one line can pass through any square, and lines can only travel horizontally or vertically between squares.
- ☐ Paths are allowed to travel off the edge of the puzzle – if they do so then the same path continues at the opposite end of the same row or column.

Re-Thinking
EASY AND HARD

Finding something too easy? Then maybe you're not trying hard enough. How can you make it more challenging? Your brain can already do whatever it is you're doing; it's time to teach it something new.

Look for the challenge. Unless you're a regular puzzle solver, you're certain to be finding some of the puzzles in this book tough – perhaps so tough that you have decided you can't solve them. And yet that isn't really true, is it? What you truly mean is you don't know how to solve them and you have decided you aren't so bothered that you are going to work out how, or perhaps you ran out of time.

All the puzzles on these pages are finite in scope, so they are all solvable by anyone who persists. On the logic puzzles, make a guess, see whether it works out and if not undo the guess and try something else. It might seem tantamount to giving up, and yet it's a major way by which we learn – children make mistakes and they learn from them, sometimes painfully! As adults, we forget that this is perfectly okay, perhaps out of fear of seeming stupid in front of other people. But in the privacy of this book, no one will ever know. And besides, the chances are that those other people couldn't solve them either!

Instructions

☐ Make sure you challenge yourself. Some tasks grow easier with time, so keep pushing yourself (although also don't overdo it!).
☐ Don't give up. Use aids to help solve the puzzles if you need them. On the word puzzles, use a dictionary or online search. On the number puzzles, use a calculator if you need to.
☐ If you still can't get going, look at the solutions. Either copy some part of the solution back to the puzzle to help you start, or work out why the answer is correct.

Week 12 Solutions

Day 1

Day 2

RESERVE REVERES REVERSE SEVERER

AGNOSTIC COASTING COATINGS

CATERERS RETRACES TERRACES

Day 3

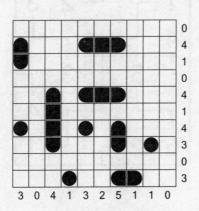

Week 12 Solutions

Day 4

Home is where the heart is

The Return of the King

Day 5

Day 6

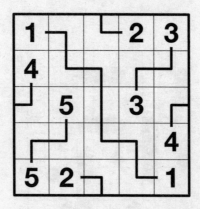

Current Brain Rank

Week 13

Total Brain Points Available: **160**

Reasoning
FOUR-BRIDGE HASHI

This variant of the puzzle allows up to four bridges between islands.

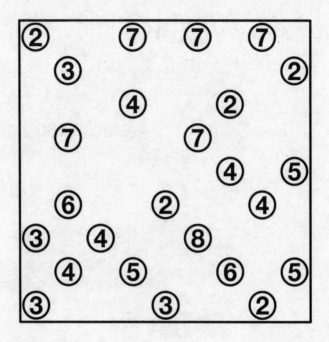

Instructions

- ☐ Join circled numbers with horizontal or vertical lines.
- ☐ Each number must have as many lines connected to it as specified by its value.
- ☐ No more than four lines may join any pair of numbers.
- ☐ No lines may cross.
- ☐ The finished layout must allow you to travel from any number to any other number just by following one or more lines.

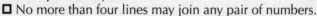

Score   Total Brain Points

Brain Points: **20**
Score 4 points per word found

Language
VOWEL PLAY

All of the vowels have been removed from the following words.
What were the original words? They are all common English words.

SSSSS

DF

RDRD

NMY

RSTV

Number Skills
SCALES

Looking at the scales, can you say which shape weighs the least and which shape weighs the most? Ignore the distance from the fulcrum.

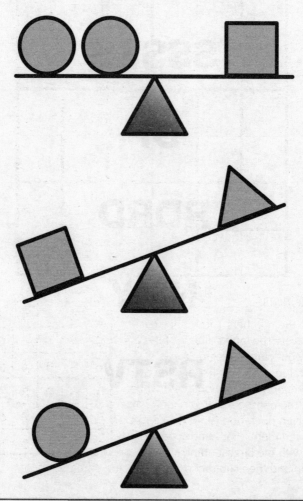

Total Brain Points

Reasoning

CALCUDOKU

This is another Latin Square puzzle, but this time the clues come in the form of mathematical constraints.

3÷	1−		6+	2÷	
	12×			11+	
9+	2×	11+		2÷	8×
		4+			
3÷		2×	1−		8+
2−			5×		

Instructions

☐ Place the numbers 1 to 6 once each into every row and column of the grid, while obeying the region totals.

☐ The value at the top-left of each bold-lined region must be obtained when all of the numbers in that region have the given operation (+, -, ×, ÷) applied between them. For - and ÷ operations start with the largest number in the region and then subtract or divide by the other numbers.

6×	20×		24×	18×	
2	**5**	**4**	**1**	**3**	**6**
3	4× **4**	**1**	**6**	7+ **5**	2÷ **2**
90× **6**	**3**	**5**	**4**	**2**	**1**
4− **1**	6÷ **6**	1− **2**	12+ **3**	**4**	**5**
5	**1**	**3**	4− **2**	**6**	1− **4**
6+ **4**	**2**	**6**	5÷ **5**	**1**	**3**

Observation
CUBE COUNT

How many individual cubes have been used to
build the structure below? You should assume that
all 'hidden' cubes are present, and that it started
off as a perfect 5×4×4 arrangement of cubes
(right) before any cubes were removed. There are
no floating cubes.

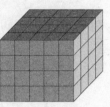

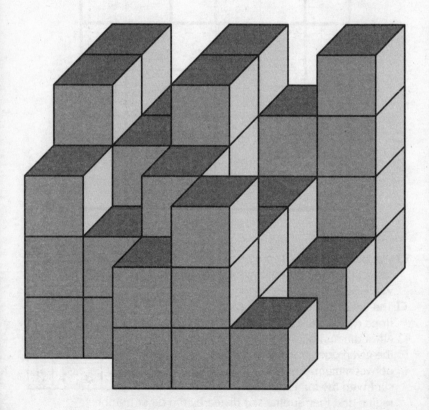

Reasoning

KUROMASU

This Japanese logic puzzle is a good test of your reasoning skills.

								5
4		4						6
						5		
	11				4			
	16							10
6						10		
			7				12	
	14							
2						10		5
7								

Instructions

☐ Shade in some squares, so that each number in the grid indicates the number of unshaded squares that can be seen from that square in the same row and column, including the square itself. Counting stops when you reach a shaded square.

☐ No square with a number in can be shaded.

☐ Shaded squares cannot touch, except diagonally.

☐ All unshaded squares must form a single continuous area, so you can move left/right/up/down from one unshaded square to another to reach any other unshaded square.

Re-Thinking

CHILDREN'S WISDOM

Adults don't take chances, or at least they take very few compared to children. Young children don't worry about failing, and they learn through experimentation.

As an adult with responsibilities, experimentation is not always a great way to learn. It's not good for learning to drive a car, for example, or fly an aeroplane, but is absolutely fantastic for a great many other things. In fact, most activities where you aren't going to die or injure yourself if you make a mistake are perfect candidates.

This is a book full of puzzles, so puzzles are a great example. The chances are really high that you've looked at one or more of the puzzles so far in a state of slight annoyance, complaining to yourself that you have no idea how to start and that the puzzle is ridiculous. Well, the puzzle may or may not be ridiculous, but you're lying to yourself that you don't know how to start. What you really mean is that you aren't sure if you can be correct or not when you start. If you just take a stab, ideally based on a sensible guess although a wild guess is perfectly okay too if that's the best you have, then you, like a small child, will learn things. You may just learn that this doesn't work, or you haven't yet understood the rules, but you will learn. And the funny thing is, do this a few times and you may magically find that suddenly you do know how to start solving the puzzle.

Instructions

☐ Don't be afraid to guess and fail, in particular where that failure will have no negative effects. In fact, don't think of it as guessing or failure – think of it as intelligent learning. That's how you got where you are today, via your childhood experimentation. You didn't read a book or take a seminar on how to walk, did you?

☐ Next time you're stuck on a puzzle, guess! You may spot patterns that you hadn't noticed while simply staring at it.

☐ Guesses can improve with time, but you need to start somewhere.

Week 13 Solutions

Day 1

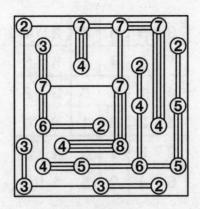

Day 2

ASSESSES

DEAF

ORDERED

ENEMY

RESTIVE

Day 3

The triangle is the lightest

The square is the heaviest

Week 13 Solutions

Day 4

³⁺ 3	¹⁻ 5	6	⁶⁺ 4	²⁺ 2	1
1	¹²ˣ 3	4	2	¹¹⁺ 5	6
⁹⁺ 4	²ˣ 1	¹¹⁺ 5	6	²⁺ 3	⁸ˣ 2
5	2	⁴⁺ 3	1	6	4
³⁺ 2	6	²ˣ 1	¹⁻ 3	4	⁸⁺ 5
²⁻ 6	4	2	⁵ˣ 5	1	3

Day 5

Total cubes = 48

Counting the top layer as level 1, this is made up of:
Level 1 cubes = 5
Level 2 cubes = 11
Level 3 cubes = 15
Level 4 cubes = 17

Day 6

Week 14

Total Brain Points Available: **125**

Reasoning
MINESWEEPER

The classic game, as supplied with Windows™. This version can be solved using logic alone – no guessing is required!

		1	3			1	
	2	1			3		
			3			4	
0		2		4		5	
1			2			5	
	2				3		3
1			1				
		1				1	1

Instructions

☐ Find the hidden mines in the grid.
☐ Mines can only be placed in empty grid squares.
☐ A number in a square reveals the number of touching mines, including diagonally.

Language
CROSSWORD

Across
1 Electronic instrument (11)
7 Circus performer (7)
8 Donkey (3)
9 Imbeciles (6)
11 Space (4)
13 Young lady (4)
14 Ship (6)
16 Poem (3)
17 Negotiate (7)
19 Upkeep (11)

Down
1 Type of toiletry item (7,4)
2 And not (3)
3 Nun's garments (6)
4 Location (4)
5 Fervent (7)
6 Similarity (11)
10 Middle Eastern resident (7)
12 Nerve cell (6)
15 Aid a crime (4)
18 Girl's name (3)

Number Skills
BRAIN CHAINS

Without using a calculator or making any written notes, solve each brain chain as quickly as you can.

| **96** | ×1/4 | +3 | ×5/9 | ÷3 | ×9 | RESULT |

| **13** | ×6 | +50% | ÷13 | +73 | ×1/2 | RESULT |

| **32** | -25% | +79 | -11 | ÷2 | -13 | RESULT |

Instructions

- ☐ Start with the bold value on the left of the chain.
- ☐ Follow the arrow and apply the first operation. Remember the resulting value in your head.
- ☐ Follow the next arrow and apply the second operation to the value you remembered.
- ☐ Keep following arrows and applying operations until you reach the RESULT box. Write in the calculated value.

Speed

SPINNING LETTERS

How many words can you make from these letters in just three minutes?

There are over 50 to be found.

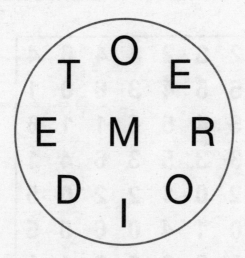

Instructions

☐ Make a word by using the middle letter plus any selection of the other letters, each used no more than once per word.

☐ Every word must be at least three letters in length, and must be a regular English word – proper nouns are not allowed.

☐ If you don't get anywhere near 50 words in 3 minutes, you can always give yourself as much extra time as you need.

Concentration

DOMINO SET

This game is not logically difficult but it requires concentration to solve, to keep track of your progress cleanly in order that you don't miss any "obvious" deductions.

	0	1	2	3	4	5	6	
								0
								1
								2
								3
								4
								5
								6

0	2	6	2	4	4	6	4
3	5	6	4	3	6	0	1
1	5	4	5	5	1	1	6
4	3	3	5	3	6	4	1
6	2	0	1	2	2	0	5
2	0	1	4	0	6	5	5
3	0	3	3	2	2	1	0

Instructions

□ Draw solid lines to divide the grid up to form a complete set of standard dominoes, with one of each domino.

□ A '0' represents a blank on a traditional domino.

□ Use the check-off list to help you keep track of which dominoes you've placed.

6	0	0	4	2	1	5	4
3	5	2	6	0	4	2	1
2	5	3	2	0	1	4	4
1	6	0	2	0	1	2	1
1	3	3	5	3	5	5	3
6	6	6	6	2	0	6	4
1	0	4	5	3	3	5	4

Reasoning
FENCE POSTS

Think about forced paths in corners, and look out for creating sub-loops, when solving this type of logical puzzle.

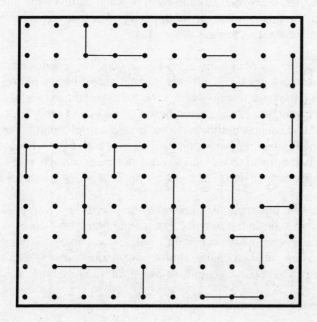

Instructions

- ☐ Join all of the dots to form a single loop.
- ☐ The loop cannot cross or touch itself at any point.
- ☐ Only horizontal and vertical lines between dots are allowed.
- ☐ Some parts of the loop are already given.

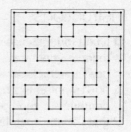

Re-Thinking
LONG-TERM MEMORY

Ancient societies used to particularly prize people with a good memory, and children learnt memorization techniques as they grew up. Until relatively recent times, most people couldn't write and so they had no other way to record anything other than to remember it and orally pass it on to their descendants.

Nowadays many of us carry almost everything we could want to know in our pockets, with easy internet access from a phone, and even the most technophobic tend to have at the very least an electronic list of contact numbers, addresses and other key information such as birthdays and so on. As a result, many of us rarely need to remember specific facts (once we've left schools and exams behind) and so we start to convince ourselves we have bad memories. But we don't – we just get out of practice at using them!

Do you take photographs? How many do you reckon you've taken, in the past year; in the past decade; in your entire life? Could you describe them all? Almost certainly not, and yet here's the thing – chances are you'd recognize almost any picture you've taken, if it was shown to you, or recognise a place you've visited before.

Your long-term memory is phenomenal. That's just a fact.

Instructions

☐ If you forget things you need to know then you're not learning them the right way. You remember stuff that your brain thinks you need to remember. Trick your brain into prioritizing things you don't want to forget by associating them with strong emotions – humour is a good one. Link facts to something funny, whether that's an unusual rhyme for a person's name or a crazy image to attach to a person's appearance. It will really help!

Week 14 Solutions

Day 1

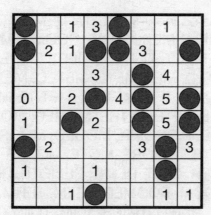

Day 2

S	Y	N	T	H	E	S	I	Z	E	R
H	■	O	■	A	■	I	■	E	■	E
A	C	R	O	B	A	T	■	A	S	S
V	■	■	I	■	E	■	L	■	■	E
I	D	I	O	T	S	■	R	O	O	M
N	■	S	■	S	■	N	■	U	■	B
G	I	R	L	■	V	E	S	S	E	L
F	■	A	■	A	■	U	■	■	■	A
O	D	E	■	B	A	R	G	A	I	N
A	■	L	■	E	■	O	■	N	■	C
M	A	I	N	T	E	N	A	N	C	E

Day 3

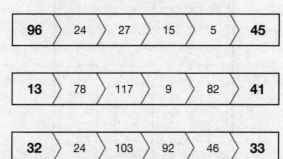

| 96 | 24 | 27 | 15 | 5 | 45 |

| 13 | 78 | 117 | 9 | 82 | 41 |

| 32 | 24 | 103 | 92 | 46 | 33 |

Week 14 Solutions

Day 4

Possible words include: DEEM, DEMERIT, DEMOTE, DIM, DIME, DIMER, DOME, DOOM, EMIR, EMIT, EMOTE, EMOTED, ITEM, MEET, MERE, MERIT, MERITED, MET, METE, METED, METEOR, METEOROID, METER, METIER, METRE, METRO, MID, MIRE, MIRED, MITE, MITRE, MITRED, MODE, MOIRE, MOO, MOOD, MOODIER, MOOED, MOOR, MOORED, MOOT, MOOTED, MORE, MOTE, MOTOR, MOTORED, ODOMETER, OMIT, REMIT, REMOTE, RIM, RIME, RIMED, ROOM, ROOMED, TEEM, TERM, TERMED, TIME, TIMED, TIMER, TOM, TOME, TRIM

Day 5

0	2	6	2	4	4	6	4
3	5	6	4	3	6	0	1
1	5	4	5	5	1	1	6
4	3	3	5	3	6	4	1
6	2	0	1	2	2	0	5
2	0	1	4	0	6	5	5
3	0	3	3	2	2	1	0

Day 6

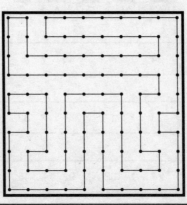

Current Brain Rank

Week 15

Total Brain Points Available: **140**

Reasoning

FUTOSHIKI

These puzzles combine inequalities with Latin Squares.

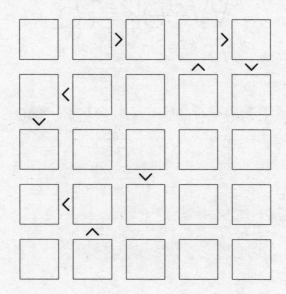

Instructions

☐ Place 1 to 5 once each into every row and column while obeying the inequality signs.

☐ Less than ("<") and greater than (">") signs between some squares indicate that the values in these two squares must be greater than or less than one another as indicated by the sign. The sign always points towards the smaller number.

Language
WORD PYRAMID

Can you build this pyramid of letter bricks using your anagram skills?

1

2

3

4

5

6

7

1. Large, flightless bird
2. Ponder
3. Stubborn animals?
4. Feathers on hats
5. A sudden urge
6. The most uneven
7. Numbers that can be divided without a remainder

Instructions

☐ Each row of bricks uses the same letters as the row above it except for the addition of one extra letter. The letters may be rearranged, however, so KIT can be on the row above TICK.

☐ Solve the clues to help you fill the pyramid.

Concentration
NO 4 IN A ROW

This puzzle is a tougher, solo version of noughts and crosses.

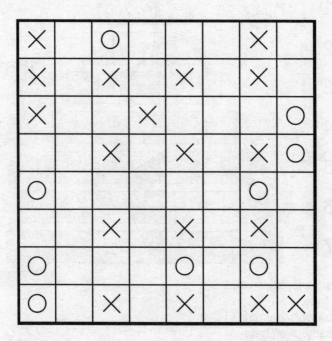

Instructions

☐ Fill the empty squares in the grid with either an 'X' or an 'O' such that no line of four consecutive 'X's or 'O's is made in any direction, including diagonally.

Observation
MATCHING PAIRS

Instructions

☐ A set of objects have been split in two, and the various resulting half-objects are shown above.

☐ Can you pair each object with its other half?

Speed
WORDSEARCH

How many of the listed artists can you find in this grid within three minutes? They can be written in any direction, either forwards or backwards.

Bestselling Musical Artists

```
R D L E S E L G A E D A N N P
L E D Z E P P E L I N R O R A
L B A D D O R C L O A T S E Y
P H I L C O L L I N S A K M E
R E N D S S S D L U I N C M L
E S I M M E E E O S E I A U S
A R I V E N O H E I R S J S E
E T D G I J Y L L S T K L A R
H V E L Y E G D T E S N E N P
A E E L N I I S O N A A A N S
B C L T O A Q Q N E R R H O I
E I I I M C L U J G B F C D V
B H L O A D C E O A R Q I A L
W U N A E C O E H L A G M M E
J D J R I H A N N A B O R E Z
```

AC/DC	EAGLES	MADONNA
AEROSMITH	ELTON JOHN	MICHAEL JACKSON
BARBRA STREISAND	ELVIS PRESLEY	NEIL DIAMOND
BEE GEES	FRANK SINATRA	PHIL COLLINS
BILLY JOEL	GENESIS	QUEEN
CELINE DION	JULIO IGLESIAS	RIHANNA
DONNA SUMMER	LED ZEPPELIN	WHITNEY HOUSTON

Reasoning
LIGHT UP

This Japanese logic puzzle is also known as 'Akari'.

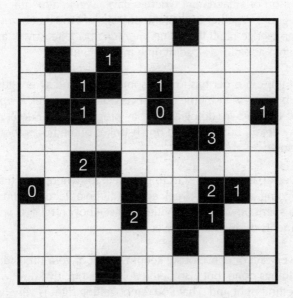

Instructions

- ☐ Place light bulbs in white squares so that all of the white squares either contain a bulb or are lit by at least one bulb.
- ☐ Light bulbs illuminate all squares in the same row and column up to the first black square encountered in each direction.
- ☐ No light bulb may illuminate any other light bulb.
- ☐ Black squares with numbers indicate how many light bulbs are placed in the touching squares (above/below/left/right).
- ☐ Not all light bulbs are necessarily clued.

Re-Thinking
TIMEKEEPING

If you don't sometimes wonder where all the time went, you're one in a million. The rest of us continually find ourselves wondering with nothing short of amazement where a day, a week, a month, or even a year has gone. Whether it's just the passage of time that bemuses us, or the knowledge of all the things we didn't do, one way or another we are often appallingly bad at time management.

Getting things in order has to start somewhere, and a very good place to begin is with a time diary. Every day for a week keep a record of what you're doing as the day progresses. You don't need every tiny detail, but the broad brushstrokes of the hours should be written down.

As the week passes you'll start to get a feel for where your time is *really* going, and by the week end you'll be able to add up the time you spent on various activities and see how it reflects your achievements during the past week.

Just the very act of consciously keeping track of your time can help you get things done, but also being able to explicitly know what you're getting right and what you're not getting right is very helpful.

Instructions

☐ Set aside a notepad, calendar or some other way of keeping track of your time. Use it to write down what you do each hour for the coming week.

☐ At the end of the week, add up the number of hours you spent on each activity. How do they reflect what you think you should be spending? Think about how you can adapt your life to better reflect your goals in the future.

☐ If keeping the diary helped you focus, keep doing it!

Week 15 Solutions

Day 1

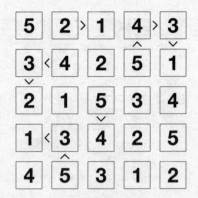

5	2 >	1	4 >	3
3 <	4	2	5	1
2	1	5	3	4
1 <	3	4	2	5
4	5	3	1	2

Day 2

EMU
MUSE
MULES
PLUMES
IMPULSE
LUMPIEST
MULTIPLES

Day 3

×	O	O	×	O	O	×	×
×	×	×	O	×	×	×	O
×	O	O	×	×	O	O	O
O	×	×	O	×	×	×	O
O	O	×	×	O	O	O	×
×	×	×	O	×	×	×	O
O	O	O	×	O	O	O	×
O	×	×	O	×	O	×	×

Week 15 Solutions

Day 4

Day 5

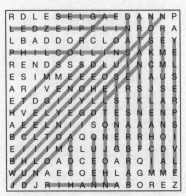

Day 6

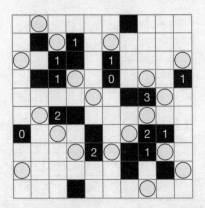

Week 16

Total Brain Points Available: **130**

Reasoning
YAJILIN

This Japanese logic puzzle combines route-finding with logical deductions based on the given clues.

Instructions

☐ Draw a single loop using only horizontal and vertical lines such that the loop does not pass through any square more than once.

☐ Any squares which the loop does not visit must be shaded, but none of these shaded squares can touch in either a horizontal or vertical direction.

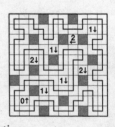

☐ Numbers with arrows indicate the exact number of shaded squares in a given direction in a specific row or column, but not all shaded squares are necessarily identified with arrows.

Language
DELETED PAIRS

How quickly can you identify each of these concealed words?

HG OA RM DE RE RE

PT RL EO DB DL EO LM

TS IE LC KM EO TM

HG EU RM DN IE RT

Instructions

☐ Delete one letter from each pair so that each line spells out a
word. For example: D̶E F̶O G̶J̶ to spell out **DOG**.

Number Skills

NUMBER PATH

Fill in the empty squares in this grid to reveal a hidden path.

	18		20			27		41	
16	15							40	43
10				2	3				45
			6			35			
			81			60			
89			79	62					52
93	92							67	68
	95		97			72		70	

Instructions

- ☐ Fill empty squares so that the completed grid contains every number from 1 to 100 exactly once each.
- ☐ Place the numbers so that there is a route from 1 to 100 that visits every grid square exactly once each in increasing numerical order, moving only left, right, up or down between touching squares.

Observation

JIGSAW CUT

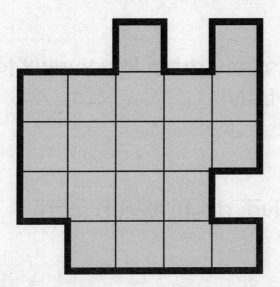

Instructions

☐ Draw along the existing lines to divide this shape up into four identical jigsaw pieces, with no pieces left over.

☐ The pieces may be rotated versions of one another, but you cannot mirror or 'turn over' any of the pieces.

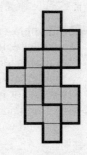

Speed
CRYPTOGRAM

How quickly can you decode these two common sayings by following the instructions at the bottom of the page?

1. Rsjvetv drbvj kyv yvrik xifn wfeuvi

2. Xivrk dzeuj kyzeb rczbv

Instructions

☐ Both phrases have been encrypted using the same code.

☐ Each letter has been replaced with another letter a fixed number of places forward/backward in the alphabet, wrapping around from Z to A. The number of places shifted is the same for all letters. For example, A might be replaced with C; B replaced with D; C replaced with E; and so on, until X is replaced with Z; Y is replaced with A; and Z is replaced with B.

Total Brain Points

Reasoning
RECTANGLES

This Japanese logic puzzle is also known as Shikaku.

			3		2		3		2
2	4		3				5		
				14					
4								4		4
				8		12			
3			24						
	3					6			2
		3		4			3		
2	4		2					7	
		5					3		3

Instructions

- ☐ Draw solid lines along some of the dashed lines in order to divide the grid up into a set of rectangles, such that every number is inside exactly one rectangle.
- ☐ The number inside each rectangle must be exactly equal to the number of grid squares that the rectangle contains, so a '4' could be in a 2×2 or a 4×1 (or 1×4) rectangle.
- ☐ All grid squares are used.

Re-Thinking
YOUR AWESOME BRAIN

How often have you heard a computer blamed for making a mistake, especially by companies who aren't keen to admit any kind of error?

Computers, of course, don't make mistakes – humans do. If something goes wrong, it's because the person who told the computer what to do got it wrong, and when people say otherwise then they are lying. And yet it's very rare for anyone to question this narrative, perhaps because we mythologize the unlimited powers of our computer brethren. But how does current computing power really compare to your brain?

Modern home computers process around 2.5 billion instructions per second, which on the face of it sounds like a lot, but the estimated power of the brain you are using to read this is closer to 100 *trillion* instructions per second. That's tens of thousands of times more powerful, and the truth is that it's more complex even than that since even tens of thousands of computers aren't able to come close to the intelligence of a single human brain.

Unlike a machine, we can't focus all of our attention on a single task, so computers excel at performing very precisely defined tasks very quickly. But you are better at just about everything else.

Instructions

- ☐ Think of some things you're good at, whether that's writing or making music or running or anything else. Write them down.
- ☐ Do you ever think that you aren't very good at something? What do you really mean by that? Perhaps you mean that other people are better than you? So what? Maybe you won't win the Olympic marathon, but that doesn't mean you can't run if you want to.
- ☐ Don't compare yourself to an impossible ideal, or some notion of perfection. Stop and realize just how phenomenal your brain is.

Total Brain Points

Week 16 Solutions

Day 1

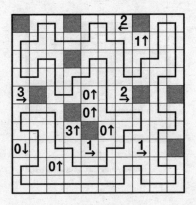

Day 2

HARDER
PROBLEM
TICKET
HERDER

Day 3

17	18	19	20	25	26	27	28	41	42
16	15	14	21	24	31	30	29	40	43
11	12	13	22	23	32	33	38	39	44
10	9	8	1	2	3	34	37	46	45
87	86	7	6	5	4	35	36	47	48
88	85	82	81	80	61	60	59	50	49
89	84	83	78	79	62	57	58	51	52
90	91	100	77	76	63	56	55	54	53
93	92	99	98	75	64	65	66	67	68
94	95	96	97	74	73	72	71	70	69

Week 16 Solutions

Day 4

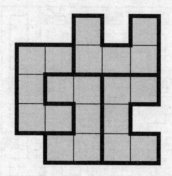

Day 5

Decode each of these quotations by replacing A with J, B with K, C with L and so on through to replacing Y with H and Z with I

Absence makes the heart grow fonder

Great minds think alike

Day 6

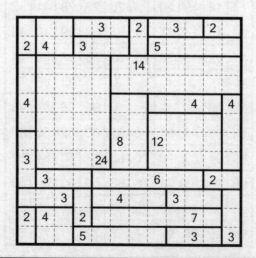

Week 17

Total Brain Points Available: **165**

Reasoning
NUMBER LINK

This route-finding puzzle requires a mix of reasoning and observation skills.

	1						1	2	
3						3			
	4		5						6
			7						
	8				7			2	
6			5			8		4	

Instructions

☐ Draw a series of separate paths, each connecting a pair of identical numbers, as in the example.

☐ No more than one line can pass through any square, and lines can only travel horizontally or vertically between squares.

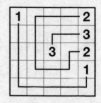

Language
ANAGRAMS

Find an anagram of the CAPITALIZED word in each sentence that can go in the gap.

1. The viaduct went ARCHING over the valley, much to the residents' _____.

2. Santa took Rudolph to the RENTALS place to try out some temporary _____.

3. The girls _____ to "TRAGEDY".

4. An unlucky _____ and one TUMBLES.

5. The UNNAMED criminal was convicted of _____ crimes.

6. He stood in the KITCHEN, waiting for his sauce to _____.

Concentration
BINARY PUZZLE

Fill the empty grid squares with 0s and 1s to make a series of binary numbers.

	0					
0					1	
	1		1			0
0	1					
1		1		1		0
0		1		0		
1			1		0	0
		1	0		0	0

Instructions

☐ Place a 0 or 1 in every empty square so that there are four of each in every row and column.

☐ Reading across or down a row or column, there may be no more than two of the same digit in succession.

Sudoku

SUDOKU

See how quickly you can solve this classic number placement puzzle.

		1	9	2	3	8		
	4	7	1		8	6	2	
	9	6	4		7	2	3	
	8						9	
	3	5	6		2	4	8	
	5	2	8		1	9	6	
		9	2	4	6	5		

Instructions

❑ Place 1 to 9 exactly once each in every row, column and bold-lined 3×3 box.

Speed

LETTER ORBITS

How many English words can you find? There are about 25 in total.

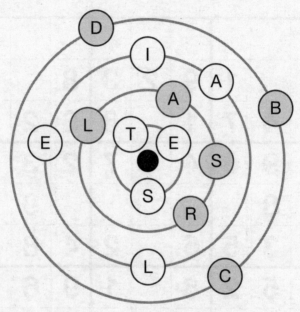

Instructions

☐ By picking one letter from the outermost orbit, then one letter from each orbit in turn through to the innermost orbit, how many four-letter English words can you find?

☐ The letters must remain in the order of the orbits, with the outermost orbit's letter first and so on.

☐ Time yourself. How many words can you find in three minutes?

Total Brain Points

Reasoning

SKYSCRAPER

In this puzzle a number inside the grid represents a skyscraper of that many floors. So a '3' is a three-storey building, while a '5' is a five-storey building. Taller buildings obscure shorter ones.

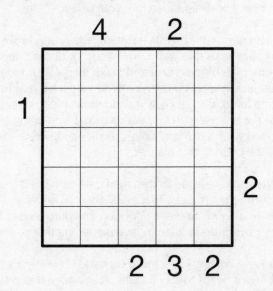

Instructions

☐ Place 1 to 5 once each into every row and column of the grid.

☐ Place buildings in the grid in such a way that each given clue number *outside* the grid represents the number of buildings that can be seen from that point, looking only at that clue's row or column.

		2	4		
2	5	3	4	1	
5	4	1	3	2	4
1	3	5	2	4	
3	2	4	1	5	
4	1	2	5	3	
2	5		1		

☐ A building with a higher value always obscures a building with a lower value, while a building with a lower value never obscures a building with a higher value.

Re-Thinking
FOOD FOR THOUGHT

You've heard it said, "you are what you eat". Maybe that was true if you were a medieval monarch, but nowadays you're far more than the sum of your calories. And yet, a healthy diet is a key part of looking after your body and therefore your brain.

What you eat enters your digestive system, where it is broken down into various chemicals that your body needs, or doesn't need. These chemicals enter the bloodstream and make their way up to the brain, where luckily a special barrier makes a decision as to whether they're safe to let in. Oxygen gets in, and molecules that encode messages to the brain also get in, which is how you know when you've stubbed your toe. Many drugs, medicinal or otherwise, work by entering the brain in this manner.

Your brain learns to respond to the chemical messages it gets, and deal with them appropriately. That's why you can develop a tolerance for caffeine, or alcohol, and even develop an addict's need for a drug. Don't let your brain learn to love the wrong thing.

Similarly, a varied diet is key – make sure you expose your body to all the things it needs to stay healthy. A balanced diet is the one guaranteed way to do this.

Instructions

☐ Have you read of certain claimed miracle foods or chemicals? These are at best guesses that seem to fit data, even for well-known ones such as the claimed brain benefits of omega-3 fatty acids found in fish and some other food. No one knows for sure of any one individual miracle food or additive, and anyone who tells you otherwise is probably trying to sell it to you.

☐ Look at your diet. Do you have a broad range of food types? Try not to have the same narrow selection every day or week!

Week 17 Solutions

Day 1

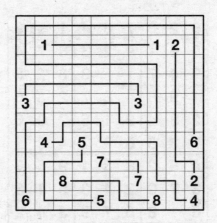

Day 2

CHAGRIN
ANTLERS
GYRATED
STUMBLE
MUNDANE
THICKEN

Day 3

0	0	1	0	1	0	1	1
0	1	0	1	0	0	1	1
1	0	1	0	1	1	0	0
0	0	1	0	1	0	1	1
1	1	0	1	0	1	0	0
1	0	0	1	0	0	1	1
0	1	1	0	1	1	0	0
1	1	0	1	0	1	0	0

Week 17 Solutions

Day 4

8	2	3	7	6	4	1	5	9
5	6	1	9	2	3	8	7	4
9	4	7	1	5	8	6	2	3
1	9	6	4	8	7	2	3	5
2	8	4	3	1	5	7	9	6
7	3	5	6	9	2	4	8	1
4	5	2	8	3	1	9	6	7
3	7	9	2	4	6	5	1	8
6	1	8	5	7	9	3	4	2

Day 5

Possible words include:
BAAS, BALE, BARE, BARS, BASE, BASS, BAST,
BEAT, BELS, BELT, BEST, BIAS, BILE, CARE, CARS,
CART, CASE, CAST, CELS, CERT, DALE, DARE, DART,
DIRE, DIRT, DISS

Day 6

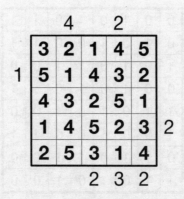

Week 18

Total Brain Points Available: **145**

Reasoning
SLITHERLINK

Just draw a loop, in this incredibly pure logic puzzle.

```
·   ·   ·   ·   ·   ·   ·   ·   ·
   1       1       1       2
·   ·   ·   ·   ·   ·   ·   ·   ·
 1       0       0       2
·   ·   ·   ·   ·   ·   ·   ·   ·
   0           0       2
·   ·   ·   ·   ·   ·   ·   ·   ·
       0           2       1
·   ·   ·   ·   ·   ·   ·   ·   ·
 2       2           1
·   ·   ·   ·   ·   ·   ·   ·   ·
 3           1           0
·   ·   ·   ·   ·   ·   ·   ·   ·
 1       0       0           0
·   ·   ·   ·   ·   ·   ·   ·   ·
 3       2       1       3
·   ·   ·   ·   ·   ·   ·   ·   ·
```

Instructions

- ☐ Draw a single loop by connecting together the dots so that each numbered square has the specified number of adjacent line segments.
- ☐ Dots can only be joined by straight horizontal or vertical lines.
- ☐ The loop cannot touch, cross or overlap itself in any way.

Language
CODEWORD

Work out the number-to-letter substitution code to create a regular filled crossword grid, which uses only standard English words.

	N
A	15 24 2 14 1 10 13 4 8
B	26 · 19 · 5 · 24 · 10
C	24 15 24 7 10 · 13 3 24 15 11
D	**A**
E	13 · 11 · 13 · 14 · · 16
F	10 24 4 13 · 5 20 14 18 25 10
G	26 · 10 · 25 · 21 · 25 · 12
H	24 19 19 14 2 22 · 23 8 6 10
I	20 · · 16 · 13 · 4 · 2
J	· · · · · · · · ·
K	20 14 4 9 10 · 10 17 14 13 4
L	· 24 · 10 · 15 · 2 · 13
M	26 25 14 20 19 14 2 22 13

Grid letters shown: A (at C/D col 3), U (at G/T col 9), H (at K col 4)

1	2	3	4	5	6	7	8	9	10	11	12	13
14	15	16	17	18	19	20	21	22	23	24	25	26

Number Skills
NUMBER DARTS

Can you hit the given totals on this number dartboard?

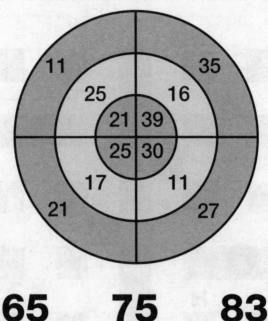

65   75   83

Instructions

☐ By choosing exactly one number from each ring of this dartboard, can you find three numbers whose values add up to the first listed total? Now repeat with the other two totals.

☐ For example, you could form 48 with 11 + 16 + 21.

Observation
SUBDIVISION

This puzzle will test your spatial reasoning.

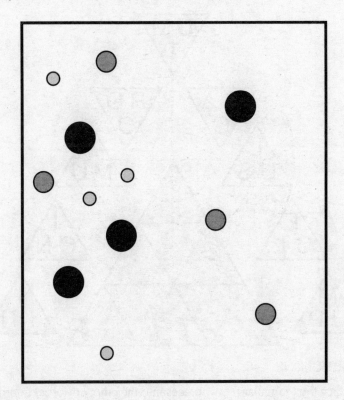

Instructions

☐ Draw two straight lines in order to divide this rectangle up into exactly four areas.

☐ Each area must contain one of each size of circle.

☐ The lines you draw should start at one edge of the outer shape and cross all the way to another edge of the outer shape.

Language
LETTER TRIANGLES

Can you fit all the letter jigsaw pieces to spell out one word per row?

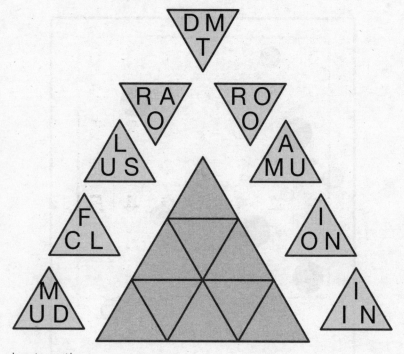

Instructions

☐ Place the triangular jigsaw pieces into the empty pyramid in order to spell out a word reading across each row. There are therefore six words to be found.

☐ Each piece is used only once and may not be rotated or reflected – place them in exactly the same orientation as they are given.

Reasoning
HITORI

This puzzle is in some respects like Sudoku in reverse!

1	4	6	5	1	4	5
7	6	3	6	5	1	2
2	2	5	1	4	3	6
3	7	7	3	1	6	2
3	4	1	3	2	4	5
1	2	7	6	4	5	3
5	3	2	6	7	4	1

Instructions

☐ Shade in squares so that no number occurs more than once per row or column.

☐ Shaded squares cannot touch in either a horizontal or vertical direction.

☐ All unshaded squares must form a single continuous area, so you can move left/right/ up/down from one unshaded square to another to reach any unshaded square.

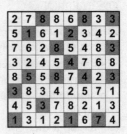

Re-Thinking
NEW EXPERIENCES

When was the last time you travelled somewhere you hadn't been before? Maybe you're away right now, but for many of us our paths remain resolutely well-trodden.

Being somewhere new exposes your brain to a huge range of new stimuli, and the more unusual the better. If you are able to do so, try to travel to countries or areas you haven't visited before. Even if you can't travel overseas, pick a foreign country and learn a bit about it.

Better still, learn to speak a foreign language – different languages tend to contain concepts not found in English, and knowing these concepts enriches not just your experience but also your thinking power. For example, maybe the language has multiple words for different types of snow, or window, or a word such as 'zeitgeist' that captures an entire concept in a single utterance. If you can encapsulate a concept in less words, it's easier to remember it and think about it.

This is also a good reason to expand your English vocabulary – learn new, interesting words. Sites such as OED.com and dictionary.com have a "Word of the Day" feature where you get new daily word trivia. Keep challenging your brain.

Instructions

☐ Think of a country you're interested in but know little about. Read about it – either in a book or online!
☐ Find out some interesting facts about a language you don't speak. Get a beginner's book and start reading it. It doesn't really matter if you intend to learn it properly or not, although it's fantastic if you do!
☐ Pick up a dictionary, or visit one of the dictionary websites listed above, and learn just one new word a day.

Week 18 Solutions

Day 1

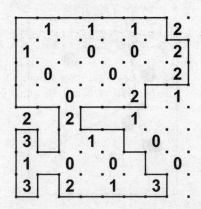

Day 2

Day 3

$$65 = 27 + 17 + 21$$

$$75 = 11 + 25 + 39$$

$$83 = 27 + 17 + 39$$

Week 18 Solutions

Day 4

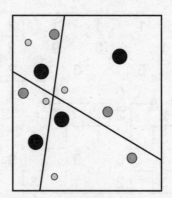

Day 5

Day 6

1	4	6	5	1	4	5
7	6	3	6	5	1	2
2	2	5	1	4	3	6
3	7	7	3	1	6	2
3	4	1	3	2	4	5
1	2	7	6	4	5	3
5	3	2	6	7	4	1

Week 19

Total Brain Points Available: **170**

Reasoning
HANJIE

This popular picture-revealing puzzle is published under a range of names, including Griddler™, Nonogram and Pic-a-pix.

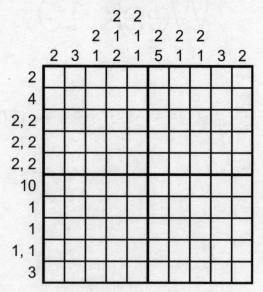

Picture clue: Useful when it rains

Instructions

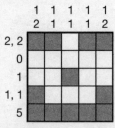

☐ Shade in squares in the grid to reveal a picture by obeying the clue constraints at the start of each row or column.

☐ The clues provide, in order, the length of every run of consecutive shaded squares in their row or column.

☐ There must be a gap of at least one empty square between each run of shaded squares in the same row or column.

Language
WORD SEQUENCES

Can you work out the music album titles and their corresponding recording artist (in brackets) represented by each set of initials? Each album has sold over 30 million copies.

SPLHCB (TB)

TDSOTM (PF)

TIC (M)

B (MJ)

BOOH (ML)

COO (ST)

Concentration
KING'S JOURNEY

Fill the grid squares to reveal a hidden path, which can include diagonal moves.

						64	
10	11	6	1				63
14			21			58	
	16		25		56		
					23	51	52
				38	50		
29		34	40	37	43	45	
30							

Instructions

☐ Fill empty squares so that the completed grid contains every number from 1 to 64 exactly once each.

☐ Place the numbers so that there is a route from 1 to 64 that visits every grid square exactly once each in numerical order, moving only left, right, up, down or diagonally between touching squares.

Observation
CIRCUIT BOARD

Which piece fits in the gap?

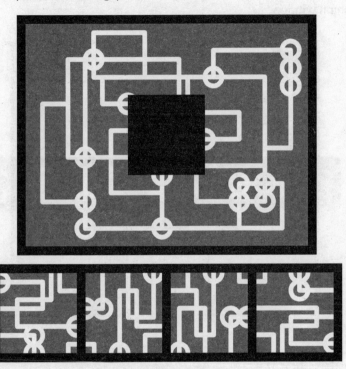

1   2   3   4

Instructions

☐ Can you work out which one of the four pieces fits into the gap, in order to complete the circuit board? Once complete all of the lines will connect at both ends.

☐ You may need to rotate the correct piece.

Speed
WORD SLIDER

Imagine you've cut out each of these columns of letters, plus the central window.

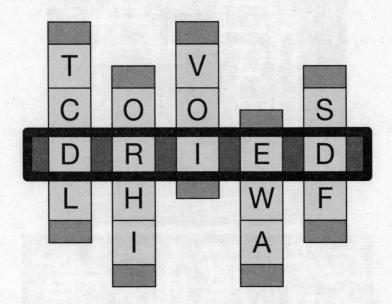

Instructions

☐ By imagining moving each of the sliders up and down, you can reveal different letters and read words through the central window.

☐ Each word must use a letter from every slider – you can't slide them out of the window. Therefore each word will be five letters long.

☐ One word is spelled out for you already. Can you find 20 further English words in just three minutes?

Total Brain Points

Reasoning
ARROWS

One of the keys to being able to solve this puzzle is working out a good way of making notes, so you can keep track of your deductions.

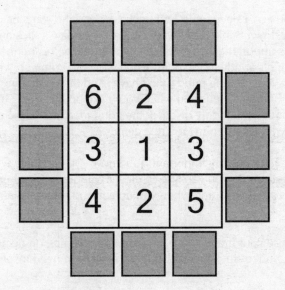

Instructions

☐ Place an arrow into every box outside the grid. Each arrow can point up, down, left, right or in one of the four principle diagonal directions.

☐ Every arrow must point to at least one number.

☐ When correctly placed, the numbers in the grid must be equal to the count of the number of arrows that are pointing at that number.

Re-Thinking
SLEEP ON IT

Sleeping on it isn't just a lazy way to put off a decision – it can be a critical part of the entire process.

When you go to sleep, your brain gets to work and starts having a real deep-down think about what went on that day. It files away what it thinks is important, and it effectively loosens the restrictions on your thoughts a little to the point where you can come up with new ideas that your waking mind didn't have. And then, amazing thing that your brain is, it tells you when you wake up by having had you dream about or suddenly discover the good idea that had previously escaped you. It's a genius. You're a genius.

Sleep is phenomenally important. You know you can't live without it, but what's more you can't be so clever without it. It's when your memories are stored, and when you do some of your most creative thinking.

Learn to use your brain's built-in powers by sleeping on decisions, problems you're stuck on, and at times when you need inspiration.

Instructions

☐ You can try out the sleeping power of your brain with the puzzles in this book. Next time you're really stuck on a puzzle, put it aside and sleep on it. Then come back the next day – there is a good chance that inspiration will have struck! This works particularly well on crossword clues or word puzzles, where your brain knows things that your waking mind was having trouble retrieving.
☐ Make sure you get enough sleep. Set a bedtime routine and stick to it, so your brain knows when you're *really* switching off control.

Week 19 Solutions

Day 1

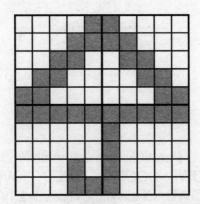

Day 2

Sgt. Pepper's Lonely Hearts Club Band (The Beatles)
The Dark Side of the Moon (Pink Floyd)
The Immaculate Collection (Madonna)
Bad (Michael Jackson)
Bat Out of Hell (Meat Loaf)
Come On Over (Shania Twain)

Day 3

9	8	7	5	4	60	64	62
10	11	6	1	3	59	61	63
14	13	12	21	2	57	58	54
15	16	20	25	22	56	55	53
17	19	27	26	24	23	51	52
18	28	33	39	38	50	49	48
29	32	34	40	37	43	45	47
30	31	35	36	41	42	44	46

Week 19 Solutions

Day 4

Circuit piece 2

Day 5

Possible words include:
CHIEF, CHOWS, COOED, COVED, COVES, CRIED, CRIES, CROWD, CROWS, DHOWS, DIVAS, DIVED, DIVES, DOVES, DRIED, DRIES, LIVED, LIVES, LOVED, LOVES, LOWED, THIEF, TRIAD, TRIED, TRIES

Day 6

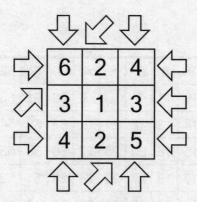

Week 20

Total Brain Points Available: **125**

Reasoning
EASY AS ABC

Place A, B and C in every row and column, using the external clues.

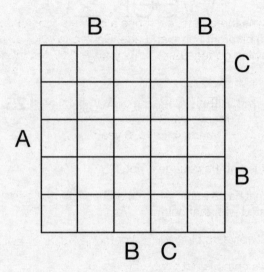

Instructions

- ☐ Fit the letters A, B and C exactly once each into every row and column of squares inside the empty grid. Two squares in each row or column will therefore be empty.
- ☐ Letters outside the grid indicate which letter appears closest to that end of the row or column.

Language
COMPREHENSION

Read the following series of statements, then fill out the empty table at the bottom of the page appropriately.

A family owns three pets, each one a different type of animal and each with a different name and age. Can you work out which of the following go together? Write your conclusion in the table below.

Animals: Rabbit, Cat, Dog
Names: Meow, Woof, Oink
Ages: 2 years, 4 years, 6 years

1. The cat is not the youngest pet.

2. No animal has a name which matches a sound commonly associated with that animal.

3. Oink is two years older than Woof.

4. The cat's name is not Oink.

5. The rabbit is not the eldest animal.

Animal	Name	Age

Number Skills
NUMBER PYRAMID

Complete this number pyramid using just addition and subtraction.

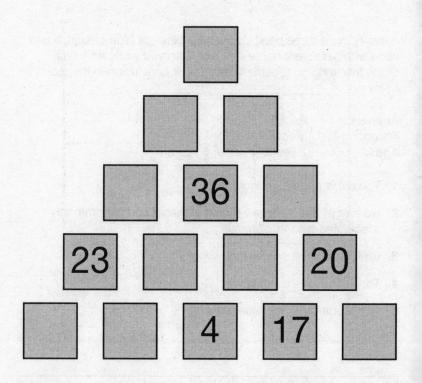

Instructions

☐ Fill in empty bricks so that each brick contains a value equal to
the sum of the two bricks directly beneath it.

Sudoku
JIGSAW 6×6

This slight twist on Sudoku ramps up the difficulty level more than you might expect!

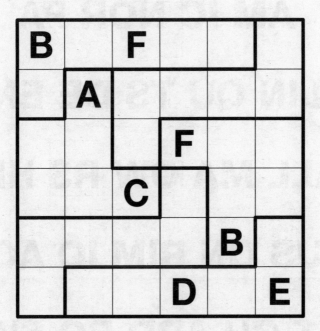

Instructions

☐ Place 1 to 6 once each into every row, column and bold-lined jigsaw region.

Language
WORD FRAGMENTS

Rearrange the fragments on each line to make a complete word.

AM IC NOR PA

LIN QU TS DE EN

ALL MA OW RS HM

US ON RIM IO AC

IT CH ARD BO SW

OU SLY OL IV FR

Score   Total Brain Points

Reasoning

NURIKABE

This Japanese logic puzzle is sometimes called Islands in the Stream.

			1					
2				2			2	
			2					
		2				2		
			2					2
2				2				
		2				2		
				2				
	2			2				2
				3				

Instructions

- ☐ Shade in squares so that every number in the puzzle remains as part of a continuous unshaded area of precisely the given number of squares.
- ☐ There can be only one number per unshaded area.
- ☐ Shaded squares cannot form any solid 2×2 (or larger) areas.
- ☐ All the shaded squares must form one continuous area.

Re-Thinking
EVERYONE IS CREATIVE

Are you creative? Maybe you are; or maybe someone told you once that you weren't, and you believed them. Maybe that someone was even you, yourself. They were wrong.

Everyone is creative. You can solve what are computationally massively complex puzzles, like finding a good route from A to B, without even realizing you're doing so. And you dream of living in a massive house or any of a whole host of aims because you are fundamentally creative and imaginative. In fact, you spend a good deal of your life imagining things that may or may not happen, and for some people that ends up as crippling horror of a thousand things that will almost certainly never happen. Those people are super-creative, albeit to their own detriment.

You might hide your creativity, or think it doesn't exist, but it does. Draw fifteen random dots on a piece of paper, and then think afterwards what do they look like? Can you join them into a shape? What does it look like? You'll probably think of things, despite yourself. But if not, don't worry. Maybe your dots were unlucky!

Often it's fear of inability that stops you being creative. Just get going, and your brain is unstoppable.

Instructions

☐ Next time you "want to be creative" start with some ideas, no matter how stupid they seem. For an artist these might be random sketches, and for a project they could be words or phrases. These can be bizarre – even if they turn out to be the opposite of what you want, just forcing that very opposite into your consciousness can help your brain bring to mind the opposing idea that is what you were trying to come up with.

☐ Write down disconnected words then try to join them in a story!

Week 20 Solutions

Day 1

	B			B	
A	B	C			C
	C		A	B	
A		A	B	C	
	C	A	B		B
	B		C	A	
		B	C		

Day 2

Rabbit - Meow - 2
Cat - Woof - 4
Dog - Oink - 6

Day 3

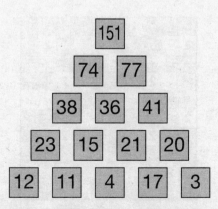

Week 20 Solutions

Day 4

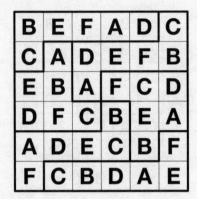

B	E	F	A	D	C
C	A	D	E	F	B
E	B	A	F	C	D
D	F	C	B	E	A
A	D	E	C	B	F
F	C	B	D	A	E

Day 5

PANORAMIC
DELINQUENTS
MARSHMALLOW
ACRIMONIOUS
SWITCHBOARD
FRIVOLOUSLY

Day 6

Week 21

Total Brain Points Available: **220**

Reasoning
HASHI

The full Japanese name of this puzzle is Hashiwokakero, but it is often also known as Bridges.

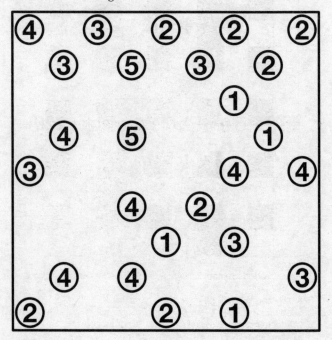

Instructions

- ☐ Join circled numbers with horizontal or vertical lines.
- ☐ Each number must have as many lines connected to it as specified by its value.
- ☐ No more than two lines may join any pair of numbers.
- ☐ No lines may cross.
- ☐ The finished layout must allow you to travel from any number to any other number just by following one or more lines.

Language
CRYPTIC CROSSWORD

Across

1 Gets enrobed for medical letters? (7)
5 A fifty-to-one boxer (3)
7 Send up parrot (3)
8 Leader left to draw up one of 57 varieties (7)
9 Swear this on account of the abandoned one (4)
10 Apparently a fruit will show up (6)
12 Keen to hold over so front runner escapes (6)
13 Gambled on a second Greek (4)
15 Name leader first (7)
16 Consume stirred tea (3)
17 Units inside problem school (3)
18 Prior routine started and finished lamentably but precisely (7)

Down

1 A daredevil with nothing arranged is wanted like this (4,2,5)
2 Circle notes generated a music system, perhaps (11)
3 Drink for a cause (4)
4 Rises after pose for exercises (3-3)
5 A short, chic lady joined men to lead accomplishment (11)
6 Crucially, try main plot construction (11)
11 Caution marketing wrongdoing (6)
14 Run away, we hear, from pest (4)

Number Skills
NUMBER SEQUENCES

Using your mathematical skills, can you work out what comes next in each sequence?

55, 66, 78, 91, 105, ?

19, 29, 40, 44, 52, ?

3, 11, 35, 107, 323, ?

729, 243, 81, 27, 9, ?

75.9375, 50.625, 33.75, 22.5, 15, ?

Reasoning
KAKURO

This Japanese number crossword is also called Cross Sums.

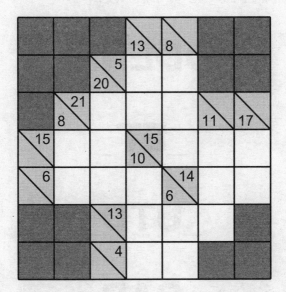

Instructions

☐ Place a digit from 1 to 9 into each white square to solve the clues.

☐ Each horizontal run of white squares adds up to the total above the diagonal line to the left of the run, and each vertical run of white squares adds up to the total below the diagonal line above the run.

☐ No digit can be used more than once in any run.

Language
START AND END

For each line, can you find the missing letter that can be added to both the start and end to make a normal English word? For example, N could be added to _OO_ to make NOON.

DDEND

_ET_

UTD

CAR

INI

AUCE

Reasoning
CORRAL

This logic puzzle involves building a fence around the given clues.

			3				3
3		8			5	6	
						4	
6	5		5				
				6		5	4
	4						
	4	9			5		6
3				6			

Instructions

☐ Draw a single loop along the grid lines such that each clue number can 'see' the given number of squares within the loop.

☐ The number of squares that a clue can see is the total count of interior squares in both horizontal and vertical directions from that square, including the clue square itself (which is only counted once).

☐ The loop cannot cross or touch itself, even at a corner.

Re-Thinking
A CRYPTIC LIFE

Cryptic crosswords are a newspaper staple in the UK; in the US, by contrast, they're rarer. In fact, to be precise there are cryptic clues in many US crosswords, but they are mixed in with the straight ones and they tend to be just a few words long and are often what a UK solver would call an "&lit" clue – meaning that the clue doubles as both a straight and a cryptic clue.

The cryptic crossword on day 2 of this week is an acquired taste. To those who aren't used to solving them they can seem impenetrable, but like almost anything else in life the secret to solving them is simply experience. The more you solve a puzzle, of whatever type, the more you become acquainted with the little quirks that puzzle setters enjoy, such as "main" referring to a sea in a crossword, or a "flower" being a river and that kind of thing. There are no such crosswording tricks in this book, incidentally!

The same applies to all aspects of life. You can encounter setbacks and problems in almost anything, but they are all learning experiences. It's easy to be sanguine after the event, but seeing problems as opportunities to learn from is not just a method to persuade yourself that things aren't so bad, but a real and genuine fact of your brain.

Instructions

☐ Think of something you once tried that you hadn't done before. Even if you can't explicitly list them, the chances are you know there are lots of things you learnt from that experience.

☐ You might tell kids that it's the taking part that counts, but the fact is it's true. You get the mental benefit from the experience, and so the more enriched your life is the richer your brain will become.

☐ Stuck on the cryptic crossword? Every clue includes a straightforward definition at the very start or very end.

Week 21 Solutions

Day 1

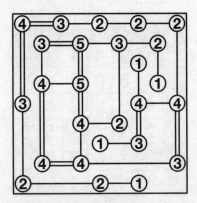

Day 2

Day 3

120: the difference increases by 1 at each step

59: add on the previous number's digits (e.g. +5+2)

971: multiply the previous number by 3 then add 2 (which is equivalent to adding 1, multiplying by 3, then subtracting 1)

3: divide by 3 at each step

10: divide by 1.5 at each step (or multiply by 2/3)

Week 21 Solutions

Day 4

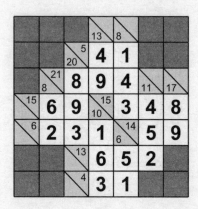

Day 5

ADDENDA
SETS
OUTDO
SCARS
MINIM
SAUCES

Day 6

Week 22

Total Brain Points Available: **145**

Reasoning

DIAGONAL NUMBER LINK

This puzzle is considerably harder than regular Number Link!

1	2	3			4
					5
					6
4					
5				2	3
6					1

Instructions

☐ Draw a series of separate paths, each connecting a pair of identical numbers, as in the example.

☐ No more than one line can pass through any square. They can only cross if they do so diagonally on the join between four squares.

☐ Lines can travel horizontally, vertically or diagonally between squares.

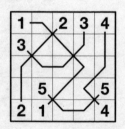

Language
LETTER SOUP

Rearrange these floating letters to spell out the names of five single-word Summer Olympics sports. Each letter will be used in exactly one word.

Reasoning
LIGHTHOUSES

Can you locate all the ships in a stormy sea?

3							2		2
1				2					0
						1			
			3						
2					1				1
3		4							2

Instructions

☐ Black squares with numbers on represent lighthouses. The number reveals how many ships can see that lighthouse. Ships can see a lighthouse if they are in the same row or column as the lighthouse.

☐ Ships are one square in size, and cannot touch either each other or a lighthouse – not even diagonally.

☐ Every ship can see at least one lighthouse.

Observation
MAZE

Find a path from the lighter circle (at the bottom) to the darker circle.

Language
LINK WORDS

Find a common English word to place in each gap, so that when attached to the end of the previous word or the start of the following word this makes two more English words. For example, BIRTH and BREAK could be linked with DAY, making BIRTHDAY and DAYBREAK.

DUST ___ CAKE

WOOD ___ FALL

There are two possible solutions for this pair of words.

PAR ___ ATE

There are also two possible solutions for this final pair of words.

Reasoning
LINESWEEPER

This Minesweeper variant uses lines instead of mines!

		6					
					3		
		8			4		5
	6						
				3	3		

Instructions

- ☐ Draw a single loop made up of horizontal and vertical lines.
- ☐ The loop can't cross or touch itself, and can only pass through empty grid squares.
- ☐ Squares with numbers indicate how many

touching squares the loop passes through, including diagonally-touching squares.

Re-Thinking
"IMPOSSIBLE" PUZZLES

Previous Re-Thinking topics have touched on the magic of guessing, either as an exploratory learning technique or for firing up your creativity, but on some puzzles, as in some real-life tasks, it can be almost the only way to get started.

The diagonal number link puzzle on day 1 is a good example. The chances are you can't simply picture the perfect solution in your head, and there's little you can be certain about in this puzzle between the finished state and the position you begin with. Instead you can make guesses to get you going, and explore those guesses. In this case it is really the only way to go, but the relatively small size of the puzzle means your guesses will be rewarded – or not – speedily enough that you can hopefully learn quickly what doesn't work and hone in on the correct solution via a rapid learning experience.

Guessing in general is a subtle art. Given an infinity of possibilities (or a large but finite set in the case of many puzzles), making a *sensible* guess is key. Look at the solution opposite. The way each set of numbers in each corner pushes out, without crossing, into mid-grid makes intuitive sense when you consider how they end up. This would be a good starting guess, as would those diagonal crossings.

Instructions

- ☐ Next time you're stuck on any kind of problem, try looking instead at what is definitely wrong and explicitly eliminate it. Then decide what is probably wrong and what could well be correct. Somewhere in there is the option for you, and unlike the puzzles in this book there might be a whole host of perfectly good options.
- ☐ When you're stuck in this book, explore a possible solution and see where it takes you. The puzzles aren't impossible – there's a definite solution or range of options given at the end of the week!

Week 22 Solutions

Day 1

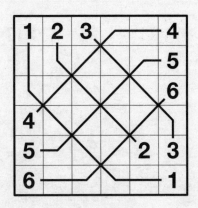

Day 2

TENNIS

ARCHERY

FENCING

HOCKEY

VOLLEYBALL

Day 3

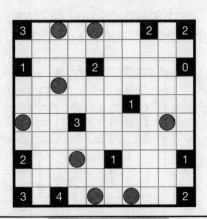

Week 22 Solutions

Day 4

Day 5

PAN: DUSTPAN and PANCAKE

WIND: WOODWIND and WINDFALL
or LAND: WOODLAND and LANDFALL

ROT: PARROT and ROTATE
or DON: PARDON and DONATE

Day 6

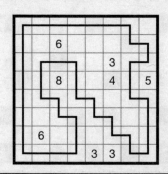

Week 23

Total Brain Points Available: **180**

Reasoning
TREN

This Japanese puzzle requires you to place blocks into a grid.

	0		0		
2		1			2
	3	2			
				1	1
		3			

Instructions

☐ Draw 1x2 and 1x3 rectangular blocks along the grid lines such that each number is contained in exactly one block.

☐ The number in each block reveals the total count of squares the block can slide into. Vertical blocks slide in their columns; horizontal blocks slide in their rows.

2		1		1
		2		
	1			
			1	1
	1			

☐ In the example, the '2' in the top row can slide up/down into two squares; the bottom row '1' can slide left/right into one square.

Language
NEXT IN SEQUENCE

Can you work out what letter should come next in these two sequences? The sequences are made up of initials, so you need to work out what the initials stand for and then find the initial of the item that comes next.

For example, M T W T F would be followed by S, for Monday, Tuesday, Wednesday, Thursday, Friday and then Saturday.

U S J M E

J A S O N

Number Skills

FLOATING NUMBERS

For an extra challenge, try solving this entirely in your head!

23   **17**

19   **12**

34 **40**

8

Instructions

☐ Can you work out which of the floating numbers above you can add together to make each of the following totals?

☐ You can't use a floating number more than once in any given total.

44   **70**   **100**

Observation
REARRANGEMENT

This puzzle is a great test of your visual imagination skills.

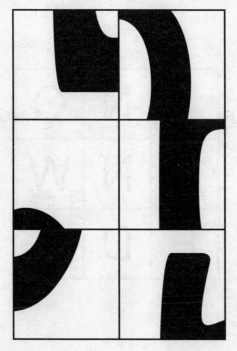

Instructions

☐ Using just your imagination, work out which letter you would be able to form if you were to cut out and rearrange the positions of these six tiles.

☐ You can't rotate (or flip over/mirror image) any of the pieces – just imagine sliding them to new positions.

Speed
WORD SQUARE

How many words can you find in this square?

There are about 25 to be found.

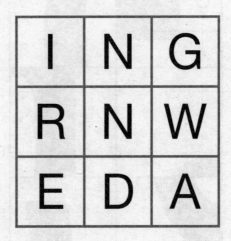

Instructions

☐ Make a word by starting on any letter and then tracing a path to adjacent letters, moving only to touching squares (including diagonally-touching squares).

☐ Every word must be at least three letters in length.

☐ The path can cross itself but it can't use any letter square more than once in a given word.

☐ There is a word that uses every square. Can you find it?

☐ Time yourself. How many words can you find in three minutes?

Total Brain Points

Reasoning
KROPKI

This puzzle combines a Latin Square with additional clues.

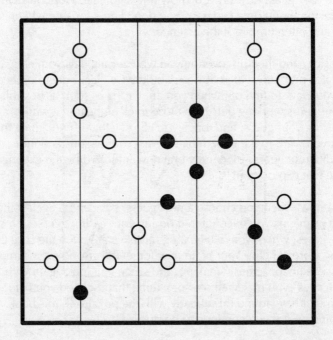

Instructions

☐ Place 1 to 5 once each into every row and column.
☐ Two squares with a black dot between contain numbers where one is twice the value of the other.
☐ Two squares with a white dot between contain consecutive numbers, such as 2 and 3, or 5 and 6.
☐ All possible black/white dots are given. If there is no dot, adjacent numbers are neither consecutive nor twice/half each other.
☐ Between 1 and 2 *either* a white or a black dot can be given.

5	3	1	2	4
3	5	4	1	2
2	4	5	3	1
1	2	3	4	5
4	1	2	5	3

Re-Thinking
MANAGING PROBLEMS

Last week's Re-Thinking talked about guessing, but once you've made your guess how do you know if it is going to work out? Unlike a decision based on a certainty, you don't know for sure where it will lead and often time is of the essence.

Guessing, and then discovering you were wrong, lets you learn about complex problems where it wasn't otherwise clear how to proceed, but you want to find out when you are wrong as soon as possible. Is your guess working out? Don't lose track of the target while exploring your guess, and, once you can see that it's not going to be what you were looking for, look to learn your lessons and move on to a different guess – hopefully one now informed by the experiences of the first exploration!

Sometimes when you choose a new guess, you run up against the same problems you encountered during your earlier guesses. In these cases, where you're repeating mistakes, it's often the case that taking a break helps. Your brain may forget the erroneous assumption you were unconsciously making, and when you look again with "fresh eyes" you may well see something that escaped you before. You might have found this already with the puzzles in this book. Try sleeping on it if you continue to be stuck.

Instructions

☐ When you're solving a puzzle, don't just focus on the local area you're working on but look around and make sure the puzzle's still valid. In a Sudoku, do you have repeated numbers in a region? In a constraint-based puzzle like the Tren at the top of the opposite page, have you made it impossible to solve the puzzle? If so, one of your deductions was wrong. Tracing back to work out which one it was can be tricky, however!

☐ If you keep making mistakes, stop for a bit and try again later.

Week 23 Solutions

Day 1

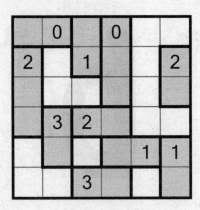

Day 2

V
Planets moving in towards the sun:
Uranus Saturn Jupiter Mars Earth Venus

D
Months in year order:
July August September October November
December

Day 3

$$44 = 8 + 17 + 19$$

$$70 = 17 + 19 + 34$$

$$100 = 8 + 12 + 17 + 23 + 40$$

Week 23 Solutions

Day 4

Day 5

Possible words include:
AND, AWNING, DAN, DAWN, DAWNING, DEN, END,
GNAW, INN, INNED, INNER, IRE, NINE, RED, REND,
RIND, RING, WAD, WADE, WADER, WAN, WAND,
WANDER, WANDERING, WANE, WANED, WANING

Day 6

2	1	3	5	4
3	4	1	2	5
1	5	2	4	3
5	3	4	1	2
4	2	5	3	1

Week 24

Total Brain Points Available: **175**

Reasoning
MASYU

This puzzle involves finding a loop through all of the circles.

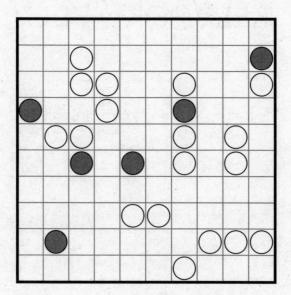

Instructions

☐ Draw a single loop that passes through the centre of every circle. Diagonal lines are not allowed.

☐ On a shaded circle the loop must turn 90 degrees and continue straight for at least one square on either side of the shaded circle.

☐ On a white circle the loop cannot turn, but it must then turn 90 degrees on either one or both of the adjacent squares.

☐ The loop cannot enter any square more than once.

Language
WORD CHAINS

Can you travel from the top to the bottom of these word chains?

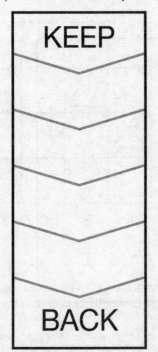

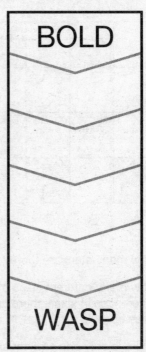

Instructions

☐ Fill in the empty steps with normal English words.
☐ At each step down the chain change just one letter to make a new word, but don't rearrange the other letters.
☐ There may be multiple ways to solve each chain, but you only need to find one solution per chain.

Observation
IMAGE COMBINATION

How good are you at combining images in your head?

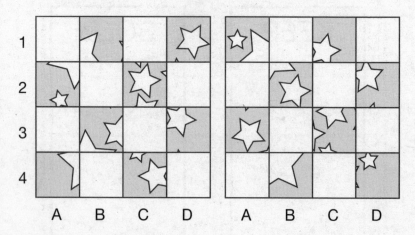

1. How many stars are there?

2. How many different sizes of star are there? There are no subtle differences in size – there are clear distinctions between the sizes.

3. There is only one grid square which contains at least part of each size of star. Which square is it?

Instructions

☐ Imagine overlaying the two images above, so the gaps in one are filled with the content from the other.
☐ Answer the written questions, based on the combined image.

Sudoku
KILLER SUDOKU 6×6

This Sudoku variant requires some simple adding up to solve.

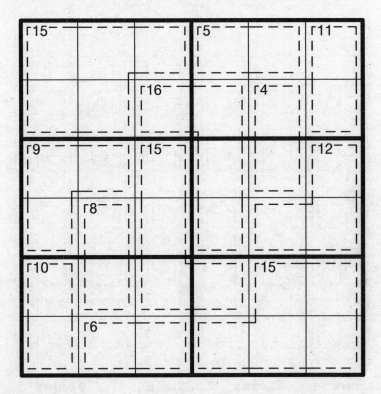

Instructions

☐ Place 1 to 6 once each into every row, column and 3×2 box, while obeying the cage totals.

☐ The contents of each dashed line cage must sum to the total given at the top-left.

☐ You **cannot repeat a number** within a dashed line cage.

Week 24 Day 5

Brain Points: 20
Score 1 point per word placed

Speed

CRISS CROSS

How many of these words can you fit into the grid in three minutes?

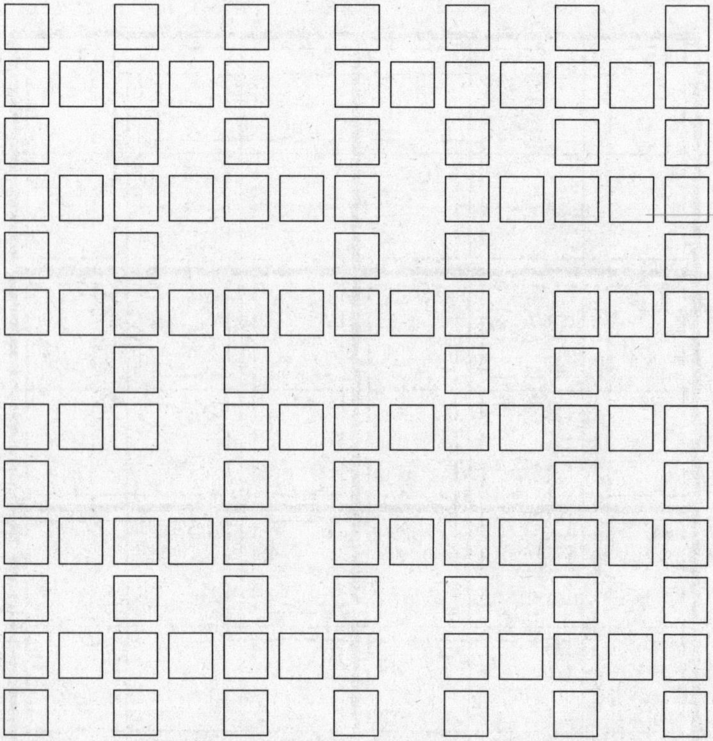

3 Letters
Cam
Owl

4 Letters
Chub
Hubs
Some
Stat

5 Letters
Bathe
Clash
Ethic
Moist

6 Letters
Earwig
Guests
Operas
Scorch
Scream
Sports

7 Letters
Ambient
Aquatic
Obscene
Rainbow

8 Letters
Criteria
Rational
Selected
Sunbathe

9 Letters
Hindsight
Listening

Reasoning
FOUR WINDS

This logic puzzle is a good test of your spatial thinking.

	5				3		
			2				
3						3	
			4				3
			3				3
7						1	
			3				
	4				6		

Instructions

☐ Draw a horizontal or vertical line in every empty
square, either passing through or stopping in that
square.

☐ Lines must start at a black square.

☐ Numbers on black squares indicate the total
number of white squares entered by lines starting at that square.

☐ Lines can only run horizontally and vertically and cannot bend.

☐ Lines can't cross, or touch more than one black square.

Re-Thinking
THE WISDOM OF OTHERS

Management consultants would like you to think they know things you don't, but, whether they do or don't, it's true that asking others can often help you solve a problem – if you know how to use their advice.

It is often very helpful to consult other people and have them comment on your plans, whether they're for moving house or buying a new car. But it's also important to remember when *you're* the expert on subjects you know about or have researched in detail, and in these cases it's a big mistake to ignore your own wisdom and place more weight on the less informed thoughts of others.

Where other people's advice comes in is often not in the advice itself, but in the new ways it makes you think about your own ideas. Having to justify your decisions in a new way, either to yourself or others, can often lead to you thinking of potential problems that had previously remained hidden. That's the real benefit of a group of otherwise less-knowledgeable people – they can make you see things afresh. Just ignore their precise opinions, unless you're sure they know what they're talking about.

Instructions

☐ You can get half the benefit of a group simply by talking out loud to yourself (or a witting or unwitting non-participating party!). When you put ideas and concepts into words and say them out loud, you trigger different parts of your brain. The effort involved in clarifying those thoughts into spoken words can help you realize things you hadn't previously thought of.

☐ Try explaining your puzzle deductions out loud to yourself – and show them this bulleted text if anyone thinks you're mad!

Week 24 Solutions

Day 1

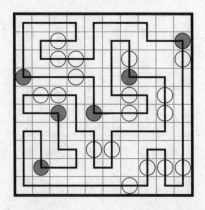

Day 2

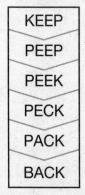

| KEEP |
| PEEP |
| PEEK |
| PECK |
| PACK |
| BACK |

| BOLD |
| BALD |
| BARD |
| WARD |
| WARP |
| WASP |

Day 3

1) 16 stars

2) Three sizes of star

3) A3

Week 24 Solutions

Day 4

5	4	1	3	2	6
3	2	6	4	1	5
1	6	4	5	3	2
2	5	3	1	6	4
4	3	2	6	5	1
6	1	5	2	4	3

Day 5

```
S   R   C   E   S   S     S   S
C L A S H   A Q U A T I C
O   T   U   R   N   A     R
R A I N B O W   B A T H E
C   O       I   A         A
H I N D S I G H T   C A M
    A   E       H   R
O W L   L I S T E N I N G
P       E       P     T   U
E T H I C   O B S C E N E
R   U   T   R   O   R     S
A M B I E N T   M O I S T
S   S   D   S   E   A     S
```

Day 6

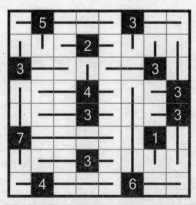

Week 25

Total Brain Points Available: **180**

Reasoning

HEYAWAKE

This Japanese logic puzzle's name translates as "Divided Rooms".

Instructions

☐ Shade some squares, such that no two shaded squares are adjacent, except diagonally, and all unshaded squares form a single continuous area.

☐ Any single horizontal or vertical line of unshaded squares cannot cross more than one bold line.

☐ Numbered squares may or may not be shaded, but always give the precise amount of shaded squares in their bold-lined region.

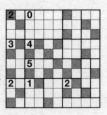

Language
MULTI-ANAGRAM

Can you find the given number of anagrams of each of the following sets of letters? Each anagram must be a standard English word, and it must use *all* of the given letters once each.

4 anagrams:
C E N O R S T U

3 anagrams:
D E E O R R S T

3 anagrams:
C E I R R S T T

Reasoning
BATTLESHIPS

Find the ships in this solo version of the classic two-player game.

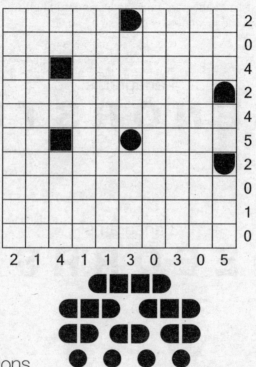

Instructions

☐ Locate the position of each of the listed ships in the grid. Ships are placed horizontally or vertically only.

☐ Numbers around the edge tell you the number of ship segments in each row and column.

☐ Ships can't touch each other, including diagonally.

☐ Some ship segments are already given.

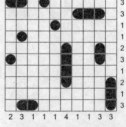

Observation
PHRASEOLOGY

This illustration represents a well-known film. Can you work out what it is?

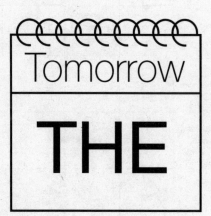

OT Tomorrow THE

This second illustration represents a well-known book. Can you work out what book that is?

T   HTEHWEIWLILNODW S

Language

ARROWWORD

Solve this crossword where the clues are written inside the grid.

Public	▼	Genetic material (inits)	▼	Specialists	▼	Mineral
Possessor ▶				▼		Extents
Deceased singer, Winehouse		Chopped ▶				▼
└▶			Golf-ball rests		Small rodents	
Receive from your parents		Non-permanent worker ▶	▼		▼	
└▶						
Teaching groups		Engrave ▶				
└▶						

Reasoning

TOROIDAL NUMBER LINK

This puzzle allows lines to 'wrap around' from one side of the puzzle to the other!

	1	2	3	
4				
5		4	2	
3	5	1		

Instructions

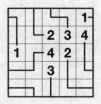

- ☐ Draw a series of separate paths, each connecting a pair of identical numbers, as in the example.
- ☐ No more than one line can pass through any square, and lines can only travel horizontally or vertically between squares.
- ☐ Paths are allowed to travel off the edge of the puzzle – if they do so then the same path continues at the opposite end of the same row or column.

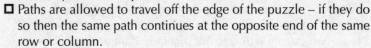

Re-Thinking
SELF-EDITING

Sit down and write a few sentences explaining what you think of this book. Now have a look at those sentences. Do they have unnecessary words that you can remove and yet still keep the same meaning? Cross them out if so, or reword it.

We all write, even if it's just emails or the odd note. Sad to say, long pieces of text often remain largely unread nowadays, and so learning the art of brevity is a key skill in the modern world. It's a place where complex thoughts become 140 characters on Twitter, and SMS messages are considered too long if they are more than a line or two.

Why is Twitter successful? Perhaps it's because people have had enough after reading 140 characters on a subject. Maybe the inventors of Twitter discovered a psychological truth about modern human behaviour, and you can use that truth to make sure your efforts aren't wasted.

Get to the point when you write.

And, by the way, why not log on to your local Amazon and put those sentences about this book into a review?

Instructions

☐ Particularly if you care about the quality of what you read and write, being brief can be a real struggle. Brevity is not always appropriate, but for day-to-day communications – or even website copy, if it's for humans and not search engines – then keeping to the point is a key skill. So practise – look back at things you've written and see how you could have made them shorter.

☐ Focus on one key point and don't digress onto a host of other issues, particularly if they're not that important to you.

Week 25 Solutions

Day 1

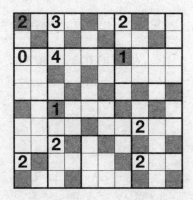

Day 2

CONSTRUE COUNTERS RECOUNTS TROUNCES

RESORTED RESTORED ROSTERED

CRITTERS RESTRICT STRICTER

Day 3

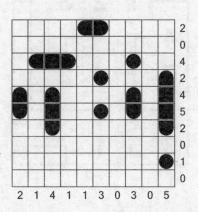

Week 25 Solutions

Day 4

Back to the Future

The Wind in the Willows

Day 5

Day 6

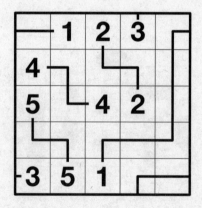

Week 26

Total Brain Points Available: **160**

Reasoning

FOUR-BRIDGE HASHI

This variant of the puzzle allows up to four bridges between islands.

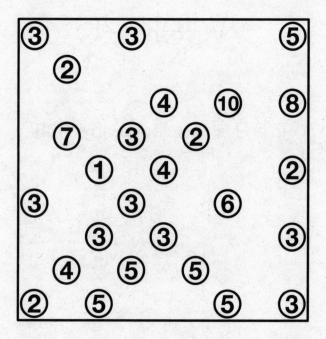

Instructions

- ☐ Join circled numbers with horizontal or vertical lines.
- ☐ Each number must have as many lines connected to it as specified by its value.
- ☐ No more than four lines may join any pair of numbers.
- ☐ No lines may cross.
- ☐ The finished layout must allow you to travel from any number to any other number just by following one or more lines.

Language
VOWEL PLAY

All of the vowels have been removed from the following words.
What were the original words? They are all English words.

NN-NN

STRNMCL

FRRR

LPL

NDRNC

Number Skills

SCALES

Looking at the scales, can you say how much each shape weighs, if the lightest shape weighs 1kg? Ignore the distance from the fulcrum.

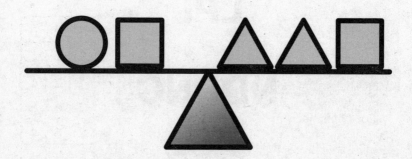

Reasoning
CALCUDOKU

This is another Latin Square puzzle, but this time the clues come in the form of mathematical constraints.

5+		16×	48×	30×	
1−					
4+			5−		8+
	10+		15+		
75×				8×	
10+				4+	

Instructions

☐ Place the numbers 1 to 6 once each into every row and column of the grid, while obeying the region totals.

☐ The value at the top-left of each bold-lined region must be obtained when all of the numbers in that region have the given operation (+, -, ×, ÷) applied between them. For - and ÷ operations start with the largest number in the region and then subtract or divide by the other numbers.

6×	20×		24×	18×	
2	**5**	**4**	**1**	**3**	**6**
3	4× **4**	**1**	**6**	7+ **5**	2÷ **2**
90× **6**	**3**	**5**	**4**	**2**	**1**
4− **1**	6÷ **6**	1− **2**	12+ **3**	**4**	**5**
5	**1**	**3**	4− **2**	**6**	1− **4**
6+ **4**	**2**	**6**	5÷ **5**	**1**	**3**

Observation
CUBE COUNT

How many individual cubes have been used to build the structure below? You should assume that all 'hidden' cubes are present, and that it started off as a perfect 5×4×5 arrangement of cubes (right) before any cubes were removed. There are no floating cubes.

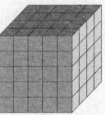

Reasoning
KUROMASU

This Japanese logic puzzle is a good test of your reasoning skills.

12	6							8	
					11				
	2						5		
			12					6	
		8							
							12		
	7				4				
		6						3	
			11						
	8							7	6

Instructions

☐ Shade in some squares, so that each number in the grid indicates the number of unshaded squares that can be seen from that square in the same row and column, including the square itself. Counting stops when you reach a shaded square.

☐ No square with a number in can be shaded.
☐ Shaded squares cannot touch, except diagonally.
☐ All unshaded squares must form a single continuous area, so you can move left/right/up/down from one unshaded square to another to reach any other unshaded square.

Re-Thinking

PROBABILITY #1

There aren't any puzzles in this book which touch on probability, and there's a good reason for that – by and large, people often find it hard, or unintuitive, to think about likelihoods.

There's a famous example of this, which you may well have come across before, called the Monty Hall problem – the name is based on the presenter of a TV show. If you haven't tried it before, give it a go:

You're on a TV game show, and you're the contestant. In front of you are three closed doors. Behind one of them is the star prize, a car. The other two have nothing behind them, and you'll lose if you open them.

Now, choose a door to open. You clearly have a 1 in 3 chance of being correct – there are three doors, and you are picking just one.

But here's the twist. Before the door is opened, the TV show host opens one of the doors you didn't pick, and shows you there is no car behind it.

Should you stick with your original door, or change your guess? And does it matter? What are the chances of winning in each case?

Instructions

☐ Read through the above Monty Hall problem and work out what you think the probabilities are.
☐ Write them down and keep them handy for next week's Re-Thinking page.

Week 26 Solutions

Day 1

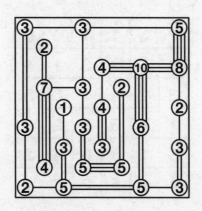

Day 2

NON-UNION

ASTRONOMICAL

FURRIER (or FARRIER)

LAPEL

ENDURANCE

Day 3

The square weighs 1kg

The triangle weighs 2kg

The circle weighs 4kg

Week 26 Solutions

Day 4

5+ 2	3	16x 1	48x 4	30x 5	6
1- 6	5	2	3	1	4
4+ 3	2	4	5- 1	6	8+ 5
1	10+ 4	6	15+ 5	2	3
75x 5	1	3	6	8x 4	2
10+ 4	6	5	2	4+ 3	1

Day 5

Total cubes = 67

Counting the top layer as level 1, this is made up of:
Level 1 cubes = 5
Level 2 cubes = 11
Level 3 cubes = 14
Level 4 cubes = 17
Level 4 cubes = 20

Day 6

Week 27

Total Brain Points Available: **160**

Reasoning
MINESWEEPER

The classic game, as supplied with Windows™. This version can be solved using logic alone – no guessing is required!

		3	2			2	
2				3	3	4	
	3		4	3			
			4				
1			4		2		2
2		3				3	3
	1		3		4		
						3	

Instructions

☐ Find the hidden mines in the grid.
☐ Mines can only be placed in empty grid squares.
☐ A number in a square reveals the number of touching mines, including diagonally.

Language

CROSSWORD

Across

1 Treaties (7)
5 Policeman (3)
7 Spoil (3)
8 Advanced class (7)
9 Bed covers (6)
10 Stitched (4)
12 Rose fruit (4)
13 Manger (6)
15 Tintinnabulating (7)
16 UK healthcare provider (inits) (3)
17 Musical discs (abbr) (3)
18 Pouches on a garment (7)

Down

1 Creating a distinctive mood (11)
2 Equates (11)
3 Reverts to factory state (6)
4 Cesspool (4)
5 Result (11)
6 Bracket (11)
11 Awful (6)
14 Part of a cloud? (4)

Number Skills

BRAIN CHAINS

Without using a calculator or making any written notes, solve each brain chain as quickly as you can.

111 〉 -81 〉 ÷2 〉 ×9 〉 -12 〉 ×2/3 〉 **RESULT**

31 〉 ×5 〉 -114 〉 +181 〉 ÷3 〉 +58 〉 **RESULT**

108 〉 ÷3 〉 +105 〉 ×1/3 〉 +129 〉 -50% 〉 **RESULT**

Instructions

☐ Start with the bold value on the left of the chain.
☐ Follow the arrow and apply the first operation. Remember the resulting value in your head.
☐ Follow the next arrow and apply the second operation to the value you remembered.
☐ Keep following arrows and applying operations until you reach the RESULT box. Write in the calculated value.

Speed
SPINNING LETTERS

How many words can you make from these letters in just 3 minutes?

There are over 50 to be found.

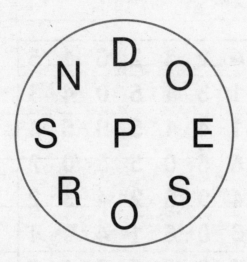

Instructions

☐ Make a word by using the middle letter plus any selection of the other letters, each used no more than once per word.

☐ Every word must be at least three letters in length, and must be a regular English word – proper nouns are not allowed.

☐ If you don't get anywhere near 50 words in 3 minutes, you can always give yourself as much extra time as you need.

Concentration
DOMINO SET

This game is not logically difficult but it requires concentration to solve, to keep track of your progress cleanly in order that you don't miss any "obvious" deductions.

	0	1	2	3	4	5	6
0							
1							
2							
3							
4							
5							
6							

3	4	2	3	2	6	1	5
3	1	3	1	5	0	4	3
3	1	4	1	5	6	5	4
0	5	5	0	5	3	0	2
0	4	0	6	2	4	3	2
2	6	0	6	1	4	0	4
2	5	2	6	1	6	1	6

Instructions

- ☐ Draw solid lines to divide the grid up to form a complete set of standard dominoes, with one of each domino.
- ☐ A '0' represents a blank on a traditional domino.
- ☐ Use the check-off list to help you keep track of which dominoes you've placed.

6	0	0	4	2	1	5	4
3	5	2	6	0	4	2	1
2	5	3	2	0	1	4	4
1	6	0	2	0	1	2	1
1	3	3	5	3	5	5	3
6	6	6	6	2	0	6	4
1	0	4	5	3	3	5	4

Reasoning
FENCE POSTS

This brain challenge has a simple aim, but can still be surprisingly tricky to solve!

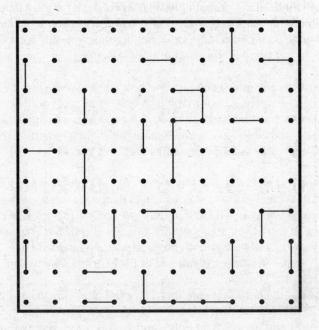

Instructions

- ☐ Join all of the dots to form a single loop.
- ☐ The loop cannot cross or touch itself at any point.
- ☐ Only horizontal and vertical lines between dots are allowed.
- ☐ Some parts of the loop are already given.

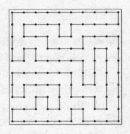

Re-Thinking
PROBABILITY #2

Complete PROBABILITY #1 in week 26 before you tackle this page.

Do you still have the probabilities you worked out for the Monty Hall problem? Many people think that it doesn't matter whether you change your choice of door or not, figuring you still don't know where the car prize is and so what does it matter?

But those people miss a key fact: the host *knows* where the car is, and when he opens a door that it isn't behind he gives you more information than you had before. At this point you now have two doors left, and while you might assume the chance of finding the car behind each door is 50:50, in reality that isn't true.

The door you picked had a 1 in 3 chance of winning when you picked it. Whatever the host does can't change that – you picked it before he got involved. So that door *still* has a 1 in 3 chance of winning. It can't change probability because you haven't changed your decision and the car hasn't moved. What happened later doesn't matter. Your door is still just as likely or unlikely to win.

Conversely, the door that you haven't picked must now have a 2 in 3 chance of winning. You know this because the probability of both doors must add up to 1 (certainty), and 1 - 1/3 = 2/3. But more than that you can work it out by reasoning:

There were three doors, but the host's action has merged the two doors you didn't pick into what is effectively a single door. Imagine that originally you could pick one door (the one you chose), or the two other doors in which case you'd win if the car was behind either. You'd pick the two doors to double your chances, and that's the choice you now have. He's opened one of the two using his knowledge, so this choice essentially gives you two doors for the price of one. It's a 2 doors out of 3 doors chance of winning, or 2/3.

Week 27 Solutions

Day 1

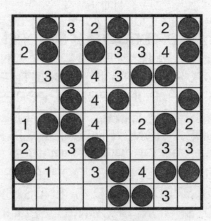

Day 2

Day 3

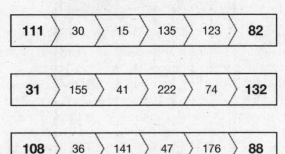

Week 27 Solutions

Day 4

Possible words include: DOPE, DOPES, DROOP, DROOPS, DROP, DROPS, OPEN, OPENS, PEN, PENDS, PENS, PER, PERSON, PERSONS, PESO, PESOS, POD, PODS, POND, PONDER, PONDERS, PONDS, POOR, PORE, PORED, PORES, POSE, POSED, POSER, POSERS, POSES, PRESS, PRO, PROD, PRODS, PRONE, PROS, PROSE, RESPOND, RESPONDS, ROPE, ROPED, ROPES, SNOOP, SNOOPED, SNOOPER, SNOOPERS, SNOOPS, SOP, SOPS, SPED, SPEND, SPENDS, SPONSOR, SPONSORED, SPOON, SPOONED, SPOONS, SPOOR, SPOORED, SPOORS, SPORE, SPORED, SPORES

Day 5

3	4	2	3	2	6	1	5
3	1	3	1	5	0	4	3
3	1	4	1	5	6	5	4
0	5	5	0	5	3	0	2
0	4	0	6	2	4	3	2
2	6	0	6	1	4	0	4
2	5	2	6	1	6	1	6

Day 6

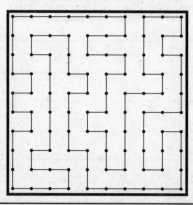

Week 28

Total Brain Points Available: **175**

Reasoning
FUTOSHIKI

These puzzles combine inequalities with Latin Squares.

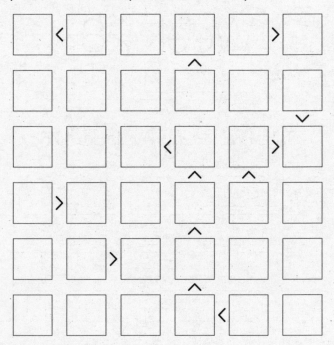

Instructions

- ☐ Place 1 to 6 once each into every row and column while obeying the inequality signs.
- ☐ Less than ("<") and greater than (">") signs between some squares indicate that the values in these two squares must be greater than or less than one another as indicated by the sign. The sign always points towards the smaller number.

Language

WORD PYRAMID

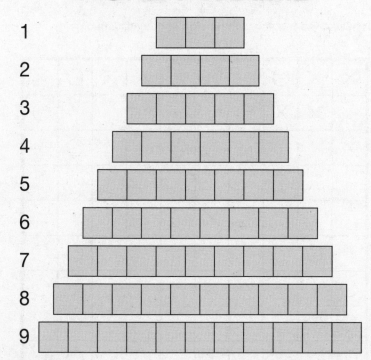

1. Feline animal
2. Cosmetic powder
3. Rope fastening on a ship
4. Medieval fortress
5. Bright red
6. Least ambiguous
7. Wrist decorations
8. Enjoys a special occasion
9. Highly esteemed

Instructions

☐ Each row of bricks uses the same letters as the row above it except for the addition of one extra letter. The letters may be rearranged, however, so KIT can be on the row above TICK.

☐ Solve the clues to help you fill the pyramid.

Concentration
NO 4 IN A ROW

This puzzle is a tougher, solo version of noughts and crosses.

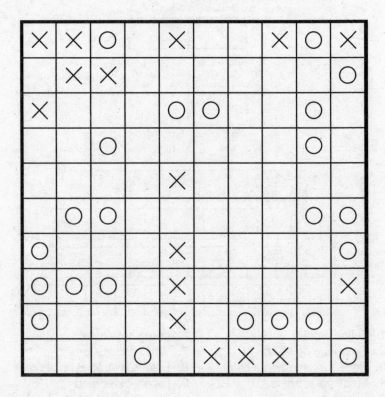

Instructions

☐ Fill the empty squares in the grid with either an 'X' or an 'O' such that no line of four consecutive 'X's or 'O's is made in any direction, including diagonally.

Observation
MATCHING PAIRS

Instructions

☐ A set of objects have been split in two, and the various resulting half-objects are shown above.

☐ Can you pair each object with its other half?

Speed
WORDSEARCH

How many of the listed items can you find in this grid within three minutes? They can be written in any direction, either forwards or backwards.

Tableware

L	R	D	T	T	E	A	C	U	P	D	B	E	S	R
C	C	E	I	L	S	T	A	S	E	U	L	A	E	E
E	A	T	C	N	O	P	S	S	T	W	L	H	I	O
R	S	U	U	P	N	A	S	T	O	A	C	P	E	E
E	D	R	A	L	L	E	E	B	D	T	T	L	T	R
A	D	E	T	G	R	R	R	B	I	A	T	A	O	A
L	T	E	E	T	D	A	O	P	O	S	L	T	P	M
B	T	N	B	I	G	W	L	B	L	P	P	T	E	E
O	I	O	S	U	L	L	E	L	E	A	G	E	E	K
W	W	H	S	S	A	C	D	D	E	S	T	R	F	I
L	E	N	I	M	U	E	I	B	A	C	B	E	F	N
S	E	V	S	A	O	S	S	A	L	G	T	R	O	P
P	E	R	S	L	E	E	H	R	A	E	B	L	C	P
E	S	T	F	O	S	S	A	L	G	R	E	T	A	W
A	E	O	A	R	T	A	O	B	Y	V	A	R	G	S

BUTTER DISH	PLATTER	SMALL PITCHER
CASSEROLE DISH	PORT GLASS	SUGAR BOWL
CEREAL BOWL	RAMEKIN	TEACUP
COFFEE POT	SALAD BOWL	TEAPOT
DESSERT BOWL	SALT CELLAR	TUREEN
DINNER PLATE	SAUCE BOAT	WATER GLASS
GRAVY BOAT	SIDE PLATE	WINE GLASS

Total Brain Points

Reasoning
LIGHT UP

This Japanese logic puzzle is also known as 'Akari'.

Instructions

- ☐ Place light bulbs in white squares so that all of the white squares either contain a bulb or are lit by at least one bulb.
- ☐ Light bulbs illuminate all squares in the same row and column up to the first black square encountered in each direction.
- ☐ No light bulb may illuminate any other light bulb.
- ☐ Black squares with numbers indicate how many light bulbs are placed in the touching squares (above/below/left/right).
- ☐ Not all light bulbs are necessarily clued.

Re-Thinking
TV SHOW PROBABILITY

The Monty Hall problem discussed in previous weeks demonstrates how poor our innate grasp of probability can be, and that applies to real TV show contestants too. That's often because we instinctively use quick shortcuts based on other real-world situations, even when those shortcuts are inaccurate for the problem at hand.

The TV show *Deal or No Deal*, where contestants must pick from boxes with random amounts of money in, is a good example of this. If the contestants were computers calculating the best decision, it wouldn't be very interesting to watch. But they make decisions that aren't in their best interests based on gut feelings, such as their performance so far, which sadly for them has no bearing on their luck in the future!

On TV shows in general, where contestants gamble their winnings for better prizes, it's often worth asking yourself whether they could do better just by going to the casino and putting it all on the roulette wheel (red has an 18 in 37 or 18 in 38 chance, depending on the wheel, so just below 1 in 2). By contrast if they're gambling doubling their money on a 1 in 3 or 1 in 4 chance of winning via a total guess, they're arguably not acting in their best interests.

Instructions

☐ Next time you're watching a TV show, consider if the contestants are acting to maximize their likelihood of winning. On some shows the exact probability of winning can be calculated, and so producers must be careful to pick contestants who won't think about this – or at least won't seem to, anyway!

☐ Casinos are successful due to misunderstandings of probability. Pick a casino game and look up the odds. How do they compare to the real chances of winning those bets?

Week 28 Solutions

Day 1

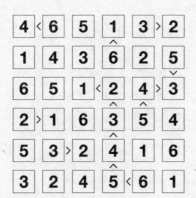

4 < 6	5	1	3 > 2
1	4	3	6	2	5
6	5	1 < 2	4 > 3
2 > 1	6	3	5	4
5	3 > 2	4	1	6
3	2	4	5 < 6	1

Day 2

```
        C A T
       T A L C
      C L E A T
     C A S T L E
    S C A R L E T
   C L E A R E S T
  B R A C E L E T S
 C E L E B R A T E S
R E S P E C T A B L E
```

Day 3

X	X	O	O	X	X	O	X	O	X
O	X	X	X	O	X	O	X	X	O
X	X	X	O	O	O	X	O	O	X
X	O	O	O	X	O	X	O	O	O
O	X	X	O	X	X	X	O	X	X
X	O	O	X	O	O	O	X	O	O
O	X	O	X	O	X	X	X	O	O
O	O	O	X	X	O	O	X	X	X
O	X	X	O	X	O	X	O	O	X
X	O	X	O	O	X	X	O	O	O

Week 28 Solutions

Day 4

Day 5

Day 6

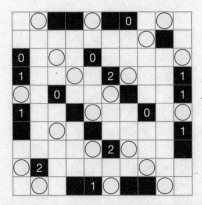

Week 29

Total Brain Points Available: **140**

Reasoning

YAJILIN

This Japanese logic puzzle combines route-finding with logical deductions based on the given clues.

Instructions

☐ Draw a single loop using only horizontal and vertical lines such that the loop does not pass through any square more than once.

☐ Any squares which the loop does not visit must be shaded, but none of these shaded squares can touch in either a horizontal or vertical direction.

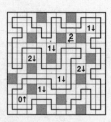

☐ Numbers with arrows indicate the exact number of shaded squares in a given direction in a specific row or column, but not all shaded squares are necessarily identified with arrows.

Language
DELETED PAIRS

How quickly can you identify each of these concealed words?

ST RE PE EA RS SA TO EL

AT RN AI CS EL AE DS

DC IH AE RS EI ST EI EI TS

AE MX OP LR OT ID DE SE

Instructions

☐ Delete one letter from each pair so that each line spells out a word. For example: DE FO GJ to spell out **DOG**.

Number Skills
NUMBER PATH

Fill in the empty squares in this grid to reveal a hidden path.

	16						1	
		25			40			
	31	24			39	98		
	88	91			94	57		
		74			71			
	77						52	

Instructions

☐ Fill empty squares so that the completed grid contains every number from 1 to 100 exactly once each.

☐ Place the numbers so that there is a route from 1 to 100 that visits every grid square exactly once each in increasing numerical order, moving only left, right, up or down between touching squares.

Observation
JIGSAW CUT

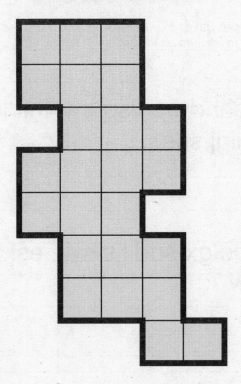

Instructions

☐ Draw along the existing lines to divide this shape up into four identical jigsaw pieces, with no pieces left over.

☐ The pieces may be rotated versions of one another, but you cannot mirror or 'turn over' any of the pieces.

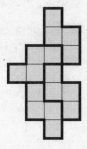

Speed
CRYPTOGRAM

How quickly can you decode these two common sayings by following the instructions at the bottom of the page?

1. Sf shhdw s vsq cwwhk lzw vgulgj sosq

2. Bsuc gx sdd ljsvwk, esklwj gx fgfw

Instructions

☐ Both phrases have been encrypted using the same code.

☐ Each letter has been replaced with another letter a fixed number of places forward/backward in the alphabet, wrapping around from Z to A. The number of places shifted is the same for all letters. For example, A might be replaced with C; B replaced with D; C replaced with E; and so on, until X is replaced with Z; Y is replaced with A; and Z is replaced with B.

Reasoning
RECTANGLES

This Japanese logic puzzle is also known as Shikaku.

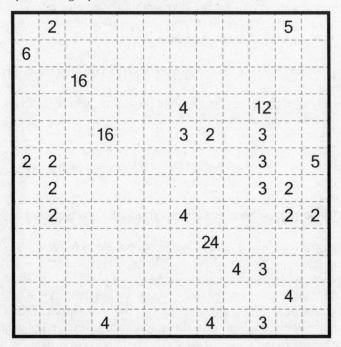

Instructions

☐ Draw solid lines along some of the dashed lines in order to divide the grid up into a set of rectangles, such that every number is inside exactly one rectangle.

☐ The number inside each rectangle must be exactly equal to the number of grid squares that the rectangle contains, so a '4' could be in a 2×2 or a 4×1 (or 1×4) rectangle.

☐ All grid squares are used.

Re-Thinking
CONFIDENCE

If someone gives a very confident presentation to a company, without presenting any doubts, it's natural to think they may well be right. Conversely, if someone gives a presentation full of ifs and buts then it's easy to think that option is more risky.

But step back. Perhaps one person has given a thoughtful analysis of the pros and cons. The other may have rashly ignored all the risks or not really thought things through. But on average whose option do you think most people will choose?

Confidence is a tricky thing. It's important to appear to have it, so people will take you seriously. And yet it shouldn't really matter, since the facts should sell themselves. But our brains are instinctive, and these cues are given undue weight. It's very hard to separate your gut feeling on these issues from your rational conclusions.

A culture of promoting bullish, confident people to positions of seniority, even if their decisions are almost entirely random, ends up promoting those who have made lucky guesses. In fact, confident people need surprisingly few lucky guesses – often their great confidence in a success outweighs the memory of various failures, which are easily brushed off as the unfortunate side effects of genius. Sadly for us, these people go on to run banks and governments.

Instructions

☐ Next time you present an idea or proposal remember that how you present it matters. It's important you appear confident no matter how strong (or weak!) you think your facts are. People base their decisions heavily on your attitude.
☐ Be careful how you present cons. There's a difference between concealing facts and going out of your way to be negative.
☐ Look out for confusing apparent confidence with the actual contents of a presentation, particularly with salespeople!

Week 29 Solutions

Day 1

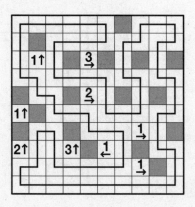

Day 2

SEPARATE
ANISEED
CHARITIES
EXPLODES

Day 3

14	13	12	11	10	9	8	5	4	3
15	16	17	18	19	20	7	6	1	2
28	27	26	25	22	21	40	41	42	43
29	30	31	24	23	38	39	98	99	44
84	85	32	33	34	37	96	97	100	45
83	86	89	90	35	36	95	56	55	46
82	87	88	91	92	93	94	57	54	47
81	76	75	74	73	72	71	58	53	48
80	77	66	67	68	69	70	59	52	49
79	78	65	64	63	62	61	60	51	50

Day 4

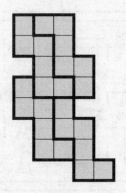

Day 5

Decode each of these quotations by replacing A with I, B with J, C with K and so on through to replacing Y with G and Z with H

An apple a day keeps the doctor away

Jack of all trades, master of none

Day 6

	2						5	
6								
	16							
				4		12		
		16		3	2	3		
2	2					3		5
	2					3	2	
	2			4			2	2
					24			
						4	3	
							4	
		4			4		3	

Week 30

Total Brain Points Available: **160**

Reasoning
NUMBER LINK

This route-finding puzzle requires a mix of reasoning and observation skills.

				1		**2**		
		3	**4**				**5**	
4					**6**			
		7			**8**		**9**	
	10							
	11				**3**			
				7				**2**
		11	**10**					
12			**8**				**9**	
		12		**1**	**5**	**6**		

Instructions

☐ Draw a series of separate paths, each connecting
a pair of identical numbers, as in the example.

☐ No more than one line can pass through any
square, and lines can only travel horizontally or
vertically between squares.

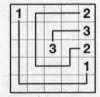

Language
ANAGRAMS

Find an anagram of the CAPITALIZED word in each sentence that can go in the gap.

1. I come to RECLAIM the world with a
    _____, said the preacher.

2. The victorious side _____ their rival's
    series of DEFEATS.

3. FINDERS keepers, agreed the two
    _____.

4. The detectives brought _____ to the
    STAKEOUT.

5. Luckily, the _____ ship was the
    READIEST to go.

6. The _____ got a ROASTING for his
    errors.

Concentration
BINARY PUZZLE

Fill the empty grid squares with 0s and 1s to make a series of binary numbers.

0							
	1	0					1
	0			1	1		
0					0		1
	1			0			0
0		1				1	
	1		1			0	
	1			0	1		

Instructions

- ☐ Place a 0 or 1 in every empty square so that there are four of each in every row and column.
- ☐ Reading across or down a row or column, there may be no more than two of the same digit in succession.

Sudoku

SUDOKU

See how quickly you can solve this classic number placement puzzle.

		5	7		4	2		
	4						9	
3		6				4		8
4			8		3			2
7			2		6			1
6		2				9		4
	5						3	
		7	5		9	1		

Instructions

☐ Place 1 to 9 exactly once each in every row, column and bold-lined 3×3 box.

Speed
LETTER ORBITS

How many English words can you find? There are about 20 in total.

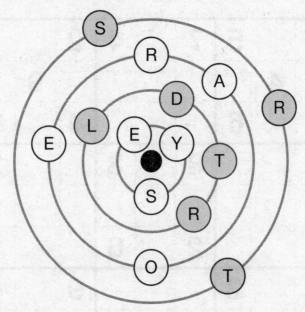

Instructions

☐ By picking one letter from the outermost orbit, then one letter from each orbit in turn through to the innermost orbit, how many four-letter English words can you find?

☐ The letters must remain in the order of the orbits, with the outermost orbit's letter first and so on.

☐ Time yourself. How many words can you find in three minutes?

Reasoning
SKYSCRAPER

In this puzzle a number inside the grid represents a skyscraper of that many floors. So a '3' is a three-storey building, while a '5' is a five-storey building. Taller buildings obscure shorter ones.

```
        1    4        3

   2 [ ][ ][ ][ ][ ]

     [ ][ ][ ][ ][ ]

   3 [ ][ ][ ][ ][ ]

     [ ][ ][ ][ ][ ] 2

        3    2
```

Instructions

☐ Place 1 to 5 once each into every row and column of the grid.

☐ Place buildings in the grid in such a way that each given clue number *outside* the grid represents the number of buildings that can be seen from that point, looking only at that clue's row or column.

			2	4	
2	5	3	4	1	
5	4	1	3	2	4
1	3	5	2	4	
3	2	4	1	5	
4	1	2	5	3	
2	5		1		

☐ A building with a higher value always obscures a building with a lower value, while a building with a lower value never obscures a building with a higher value.

Re-Thinking
FALSE PERSUASION

Have you ever been swayed by a sales promotion? Do those 50% off stickers get you buying things you don't really want, and would never have bought otherwise?

This brings up two issues. Firstly, why would you buy something you didn't really want? But secondly, how do you know the offers are genuine in the first place? Often you don't, but the risk of missing out makes you feel inclined to buy the product anyway.

Your brain takes false shortcuts, based on past experience. You want to save money – here, you can save money! The price is a different colour; it must be special! Your brain responds to the same stimuli that have excited you in the past, but it is a basic response that sometimes you need to override. All you *know* is the price itself. Maybe you can somehow check if it's a real saving, but if not then ignore the claimed discount and decide whether you want it based on the price itself, not the alleged discount. Use rational thinking.

Another sales technique is applying pressure to make a quick decision. If someone tells you you are going to miss out, they care about losing your sale. This must mean they aren't at all certain to sell it to anyone else, so you have time to go away and think. Probably they know that if you think about it you won't want it.

Instructions

- ☐ Almost all stores discount products from time to time, and in some stores the discount price is the "real" price – they don't expect to sell at the higher price.
- ☐ In some cases discounts can be shown when the product literally never sold at a higher price. Don't trust them unless you *know* they are true. They are exploiting your brain's weaknesses!
- ☐ Don't be swayed by a salesperson. If you feel even a tiny bit of pressure to buy, don't. It's a warning sign that you should rethink!

Week 30 Solutions

Day 1

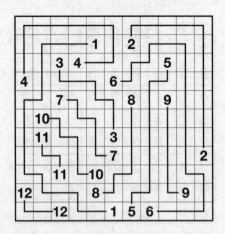

Day 2

MIRACLE
FEASTED
FRIENDS
TAKEOUTS
STEADIER
ORGANIST

Day 3

0	0	1	0	1	0	1	1
0	1	0	1	0	0	1	1
1	0	1	0	1	1	0	0
0	0	1	0	1	0	1	1
1	1	0	1	0	1	0	0
0	0	1	0	1	0	1	1
1	1	0	1	0	1	0	0
1	1	0	1	0	1	0	0

Week 30 Solutions

Day 4

1	9	5	7	8	4	2	6	3
2	4	8	6	3	1	7	9	5
3	7	6	9	2	5	4	1	8
4	6	1	8	9	3	5	7	2
5	2	3	4	1	7	6	8	9
7	8	9	2	5	6	3	4	1
6	1	2	3	7	8	9	5	4
9	5	4	1	6	2	8	3	7
8	3	7	5	4	9	1	2	6

Day 5

Possible words include:
RADS, RARE, RATE, RATS, REDS, RELY, RODE,
RODS, ROLE, ROTE, ROTS, SALE, SATE, SERE, SETS,
SODS, SOLE, SOLS, SORE, SOTS, TADS, TALE, TARE,
TARS, TATS, TODS, TORE, TORS, TOTE, TOTS

Day 6

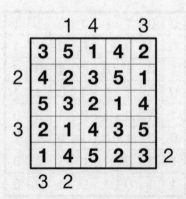

Week 31

Total Brain Points Available: **155**

Reasoning
SLITHERLINK

Just draw a loop, in this incredibly pure logic puzzle.

```
.   .   .   .   .   .   .   .
   3       2       3   3
.   .   .   .   .   .   .   .
  2  2               2       3
.   .   .   .   .   .   .   .
      2       2       3       2
.   .   .   .   .   .   .   .
  2   3   3   2
.   .   .   .   .   .   .   .
                  1   1   3   3
.   .   .   .   .   .   .   .
  2       3       3       2
.   .   .   .   .   .   .   .
  3       3               1   3
.   .   .   .   .   .   .   .
     0   2       2       2
.   .   .   .   .   .   .   .
```

Instructions

☐ Draw a single loop by connecting together the dots so that each numbered square has the specified number of adjacent line segments.

☐ Dots can only be joined by straight horizontal or vertical lines.

☐ The loop cannot touch, cross or overlap itself in any way.

Language

CODEWORD

Work out the number-to-letter substitution code to create a regular filled crossword grid, which uses only standard English words.

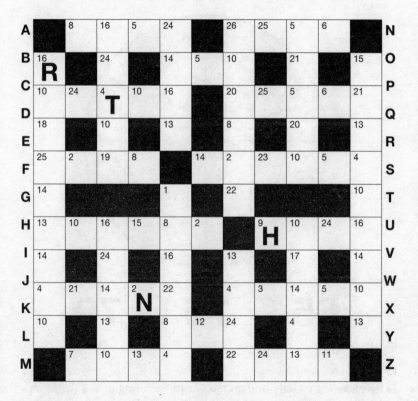

Number Skills
NUMBER DARTS

Can you hit the given totals on this number dartboard?

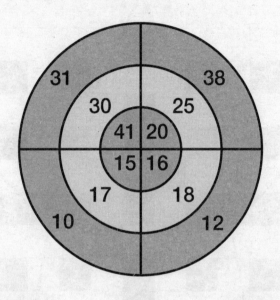

65   **75**   **79**

Instructions
☐ By choosing exactly one number from each ring of this dartboard, can you find three numbers whose values add up to the first listed total? Now repeat with the other two totals.
☐ For example, you could form 60 with 10 + 30 + 20.

Observation

SUBDIVISION

This puzzle will test your spatial reasoning.

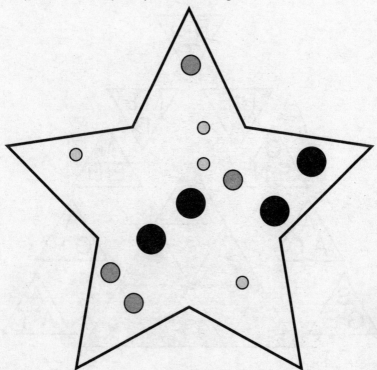

Instructions

☐ Draw three straight lines in order to divide this star up into exactly four areas.

☐ Each area must contain one of each size of circle.

☐ The lines you draw should start at one edge of the star, and not cross any other line you draw. They may end either at another edge of the star or when they reach another line.

☐ Lines may not travel outside the edges of the star.

Language
LETTER TRIANGLES

Can you fit all the letter jigsaw pieces to spell out one word per row?

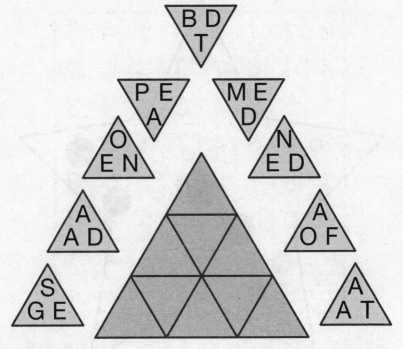

Instructions

☐ Place the triangular jigsaw pieces into the empty pyramid in order to spell out a word reading across each row. There are therefore six words to be found.

☐ Each piece is used only once and may not be rotated or reflected – place them in exactly the same orientation as they are given.

Reasoning

HITORI

This puzzle is in some respects like Sudoku in reverse!

8	2	1	5	3	5	4	5
4	4	6	7	8	3	2	2
1	5	7	4	2	2	6	3
3	4	5	4	7	1	8	6
1	8	7	2	4	7	5	3
7	6	3	6	8	5	8	8
2	7	4	8	5	1	2	1
5	6	2	1	2	4	8	4

Instructions

☐ Shade in squares so that no number occurs
more than once per row or column.

☐ Shaded squares cannot touch in either a
horizontal or vertical direction.

☐ All unshaded squares must form a single
continuous area, so you can move left/right/
up/down from one unshaded square to
another to reach any unshaded square.

2	7	8	8	6	8	3	3
5	1	6	1	2	3	4	2
7	6	2	8	5	4	8	3
3	2	4	5	4	7	6	8
8	5	5	8	7	4	2	3
3	8	3	4	2	5	7	1
4	5	3	7	8	2	1	3
1	3	1	2	1	6	7	4

Re-Thinking

COLOURED PERCEPTION

Some people associate days of the week with colours. They can't help it – it's called synaesthesia. More generally, we all associate things that don't actually go together. We also can't help it, but if we know it happens we can at least make allowance for it.

Imagine you have just met someone with the same name as another person you know, but don't really like. Do you unwittingly associate some of the characteristics of that other person with the new person you just met? It's not rational, but your brain only has the name to go on and existing strong feelings about that name are enough to rub off on the next person. The effect should go away as you get to know them, but you can't help your initial reaction.

The same applies to all kinds of emotions. Something you already enjoy can be "spoiled" for you by a later association with something negative – these can seem silly or trivial when you describe them, but they feel real, and they (metaphorically!) colour our later perceptions. For example, perhaps the manufacturer of your favourite coffee maker turns out to have really bad customer service, and suddenly the coffees you have always enjoyed don't seem so great! It doesn't really make sense, but it's hard to separate the emotions connected to the coffee maker from the drinks it produces.

Instructions

☐ Look out for irrelevant inferences in your everyday life. When you rush to judgement about someone or something, see if you can work out why you think that way.

☐ Although inferences can be misleading, they're also often very helpful. Sometimes you'll detect small patterns of behaviour without even realizing explicitly what they are, and these can alert you to potentially unsafe situations. You may get some false associations, but the general mechanism is very important!

Week 31 Solutions

Day 1

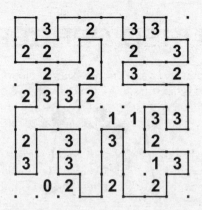

Day 2

Day 3

$$65 = 31 + 18 + 16$$

$$75 = 38 + 17 + 20$$

$$79 = 38 + 25 + 16$$

Week 31 Solutions

Day 4

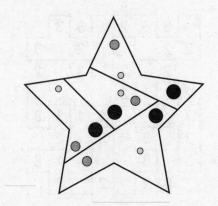

Day 5

Day 6

8	2	1	5	3	5	4	5
4	4	6	7	8	3	2	2
1	5	7	4	2	2	6	3
3	4	5	4	7	1	8	6
1	8	7	2	4	7	5	3
7	6	3	6	8	5	8	8
2	7	4	8	5	1	2	1
5	6	2	1	2	4	8	4

Week 32

Total Brain Points Available: **165**

Reasoning

HANJIE

This popular picture-revealing puzzle is published under a range of names, including Griddler™, Nonogram and Pic-a-pix.

		2	3		1	3	2			
		2	1	5	3	1	2			
	2	4	2	1	1	1	1	2	4	2
6										
3, 2										
4										
2										
6										
2, 2										
2, 2										
2, 2										
2, 2										
6										

Picture clue: Diamond?

Instructions

- Shade in squares in the grid to reveal a picture by obeying the clue constraints at the start of each row or column.
- The clues provide, in order, the length of every run of consecutive shaded squares in their row or column.
- There must be a gap of at least one empty square between each run of shaded squares in the same row or column.

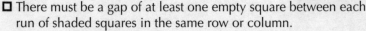

	1 2	1 1	1 1	1 1	1 2
2, 2					
0					
1					
1, 1					
5					

Language
WORD SEQUENCES

Can you work out the film titles represented by each set of initials?
Each film has had a worldwide gross in excess of $750 million.

TDOTM

POTCDMC

IJATKOTCS

THAUJ

ETTET

TLK

Concentration
KING'S JOURNEY

Fill the grid squares to reveal a hidden path, which can include diagonal moves.

5		17			21		
	6			20	23	27	25
			13				28
	10	1				31	44
				33			
		59					41
		54		64	35	37	
56			63				39

Instructions

☐ Fill empty squares so that the completed grid contains every number from 1 to 64 exactly once each.
☐ Place the numbers so that there is a route from 1 to 64 that visits every grid square exactly once each in numerical order, moving only left, right, up, down or diagonally between touching squares.

Observation
CIRCUIT BOARD

Which piece fits in the gap?

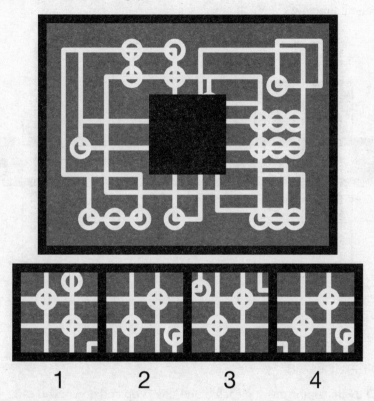

| 1 | 2 | 3 | 4 |

Instructions

☐ Can you work out which one of the four pieces fits into the gap, in order to complete the circuit board? Once complete all of the lines will connect at both ends.

☐ You may need to rotate the correct piece.

Speed
WORD SLIDER

Imagine you've cut out each of these columns of letters, plus the central window.

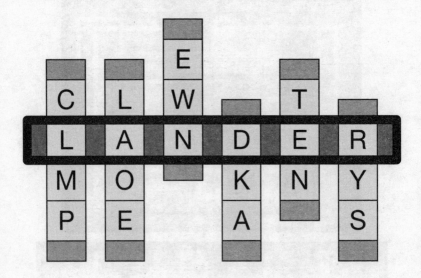

Instructions

- ☐ By imagining moving each of the sliders up and down, you can reveal different letters and read words through the central window.
- ☐ Each word must use a letter from every slider – you can't slide them out of the window. Therefore each word will be six letters long.
- ☐ One word is spelled out for you already. Can you find 10 further English words in just three minutes?

Reasoning
ARROWS

One of the keys to being able to solve this puzzle is working out a
good way of making notes, so you can keep track of your deductions.

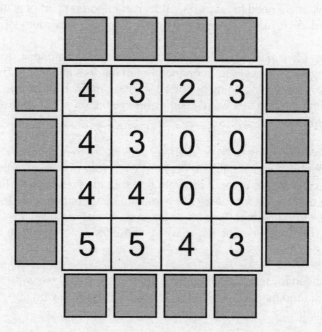

Instructions

- ☐ Place an arrow into every box outside the
  grid. Each arrow can point up, down, left,
  right or in one of the four principle diagonal
  directions.
- ☐ Every arrow must point to at least one number.
- ☐ When correctly placed, the numbers in the
  grid must be equal to the count of the number of arrows that are
  pointing at that number.

Re-Thinking
DISTRACTIONS

Some of us can work in very noisy environments, while others need peace and quiet. But by and large we all have things that distract us from what we need to focus on, and so an important part of getting things done is making sure that we have a suitable environment.

Modern life is packed full of distractions, from ringing phones to beeping text messages to permanently-full inboxes and so on. There is always something going on, or a TV left on in the background, or an online bargain that we're keeping an eye on, or any of a massive host of things.

When you're trying to be productive, actively try to minimize distractions. If you are able to do so, silence your phone, or at the very least close your email program and shut the web browser (if you're not using it for research!). If you are in a separate room to others, close the door. Turn off distracting sources of noise, if you can. Consciously decide not to worry about the other tasks you have to do.

If you need to, set aside a chunk of time where you agree with yourself (and maybe even others) in advance that you won't be disturbed.

Instructions

☐ When we are disturbed, we tend to lose our train of thought and often we then succumb to a series of other distractions and put off the productive part of our day for far too long. As a first step, when you *are* disturbed make a conscious decision to get back to your important task as soon as possible.
☐ Think about how you can minimize distractions. Sometimes you can rotate your screen or chair to a different angle with less distractions, or you can switch off non-critical electronic alerts.

Week 32 Solutions

Day 1

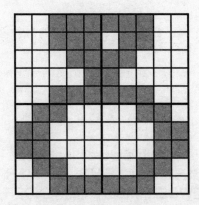

Day 2

Transformers: Dark of the Moon
Pirates of the Caribbean: Dead Man's Chest
Indiana Jones and the Kingdom of the Crystal Skull
The Hobbit: An Unexpected Journey
E. T. The Extra-Terrestrial
The Lion King

Day 3

5	4	17	19	22	21	24	26
3	6	18	16	20	23	27	25
7	2	11	13	15	30	29	28
8	10	1	12	14	32	31	44
9	50	49	48	33	46	45	43
51	58	59	60	47	34	42	41
57	52	54	61	64	35	37	40
56	55	53	63	62	36	38	39

Date Completed

Week 32 Solutions

Day 4

Circuit piece 4

Day 5

Possible words include:
CANKER, CLEANS, CLEATS, CONKER, LANDER,
LENDER, LEWDER, MEEKER, MENDER, MONKEY,
PAEANS, PANDER, PLEATS, PONDER, POWDER

Day 6

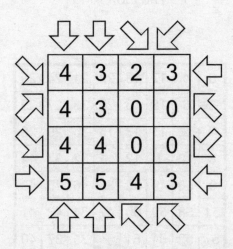

Week 33

Total Brain Points Available: **140**

Reasoning

EASY AS ABC

Place A, B and C in every row and column, using the external clues.

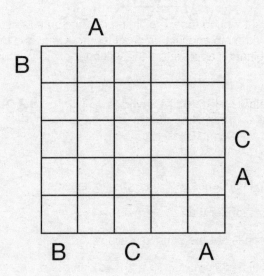

Instructions

☐ Fit the letters A, B and C exactly once each into every row and column of squares inside the empty grid. Two squares in each row or column will therefore be empty.

☐ Letters outside the grid indicate which letter appears closest to that end of the row or column.

Language
COMPREHENSION

Read the following series of statements, then fill out the empty table at the bottom of the page appropriately.

Three different writing tools are sitting on the same table. Each has a different width nib and is a different length. Can you work out which combination applies to each writing tool?

Writing tools: Pen, Pencil, Crayon
Nib widths: 1mm, 4mm, 5mm
Lengths: 8cm, 10cm, 12cm

1. One item is 30 times as long as its nib is wide.

2. The pen is longer than the pencil.

3. The crayon is not the longest writing tool.

4. The pencil has a smaller nib than the pen does.

5. The 1mm nib is not used by the 8cm-long writing tool.

Writing tool	Nib width	Length

Number Skills
NUMBER PYRAMID

Complete this number pyramid using just addition and subtraction.

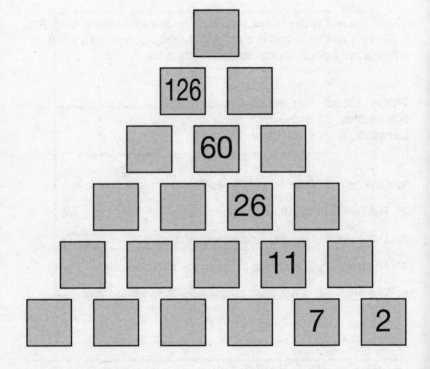

Instructions

☐ Fill in empty bricks so that each brick contains a value equal to the sum of the two bricks directly beneath it.

Total Brain Points

Sudoku
JIGSAW 7×7

This jigsaw twist on Sudoku ramps up the difficulty level more than you might expect!

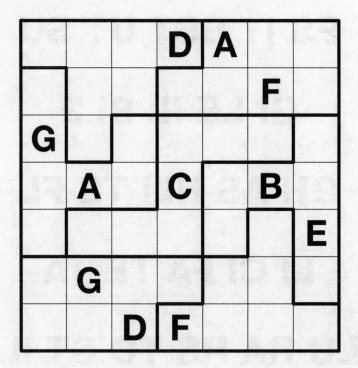

Instructions

☐ Place 1 to 7 once each into every row, column and bold-lined jigsaw region.

Language
WORD FRAGMENTS

Rearrange the fragments on each line to make a complete word.

ES IT BST UT SU

GI LE IL BLE

GH AS HLI TS FL

LI CI FA TE TA

LU RA RS TO ST IL

ER OG PH RA BI

Reasoning
NURIKABE

This Japanese logic puzzle is sometimes called Islands in the Stream.

									1
	1								
		2		8			1		
	3						3		
		4						6	
		7			2		3		
								1	
4									

Instructions

☐ Shade in squares so that every number in the puzzle remains as part of a continuous unshaded area of precisely the given number of squares.

☐ There can be only one number per unshaded area.

☐ Shaded squares cannot form any solid 2×2 (or larger) areas.

☐ All the shaded squares must form one continuous area.

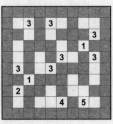

Re-Thinking
MEMORY TECHNIQUES

Lots of techniques exist for improving your long-term memory. Entire books have been written on them, and some of them require serious effort to learn and apply, but there are also plenty of basic techniques that you can use when you need to reliably memorize information.

Ridiculous things are particularly memorable – they seem novel to our brains, and so it pays attention. If you want to remember a series of items, link them together in a ridiculous way. If you need to buy cabbage, eggs and bread, for example, these are so mundane you might well forget the list by the time you're in the supermarket. But if you imagine the cabbage with eggs growing out of the centre, and bread cracking out of the cabbage-eggs when you break them, it's pretty hard to forget them – at least for a few hours, anyway!

The same kind of ridiculous association can be used to remember all kinds of things, and you can extend it to learning not just sets but also sequences. If you learn in advance a series of things in sequence, such as rooms you pass through in a building, then if you associate the objects with those rooms as you imagine walking through the building, you will recall not only the objects but the order they're in. That takes effort in advance, but you can re-use the prelearnt sequence time and time again!

Instructions

☐ Next time you go shopping try memorizing what you want to buy by using ridiculous associations between objects – the more creative, bizarre and funny the better!
☐ Think about how you walk through a large building you know well. Practise associating objects with things you know are in those rooms already. Once your mental building is well known to you, start inventing extra rooms. It will come in useful one day!

Week 33 Solutions

Day 1

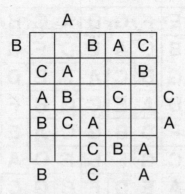

Day 2

Pencil - 1mm - 10cm
Pen - 4mm - 12cm
Crayon - 5mm - 8cm

Day 3

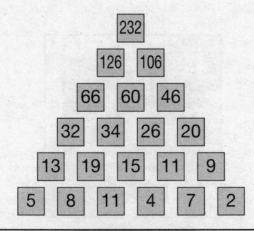

Day 4

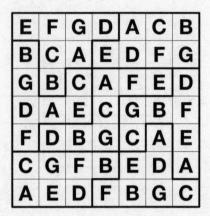

Day 5

SUBSTITUTES
ILLEGIBLE
FLASHLIGHTS
FACILITATE
ILLUSTRATORS
BIOGRAPHER

Day 6

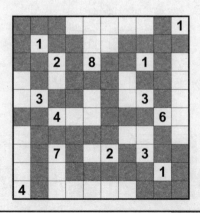

Week 34

Total Brain Points Available: **235**

Reasoning

HASHI

The full Japanese name of this puzzle is Hashiwokakero, but it is often also known as Bridges.

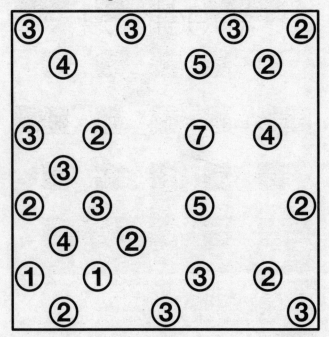

Instructions

- ☐ Join circled numbers with horizontal or vertical lines.
- ☐ Each number must have as many lines connected to it as specified by its value.
- ☐ No more than two lines may join any pair of numbers.
- ☐ No lines may cross.
- ☐ The finished layout must allow you to travel from any number to any other number just by following one or more lines.

Language

CRYPTIC CROSSWORD

Across

1 Nice places to arrange your pens in? (6,4)
5 Turned stone over to find messages (5)
7 Poultry initially sets down frolics (5)
9 A desire was settled upon (6)
10 Change turns the tide (4)
12 Are ear sounds tuneful? (4)
13 Ghost pixie gained one but lost energy (6)
16 Divide initial sale holdings and reallocate earnings (5)
17 Catches late birds in their homes (5)
18 Advises about common repairs (10)

Down

1 Black and white animal and hugged by father (5)
2 Released 500th edition (6)
3 A duplicate policeman variable (4)
4 Benchmarks flags (9)
6 Abort - semester in A-team cut in half (9)
8 Scheduled a group (3)
11 Derived name from European patent office state mark (6)
12 Pauses, even for a fool (3)
14 Hardy heroine holding first ticket for trials (5)
15 Woman's old champion (4)

Number Skills

NUMBER SEQUENCES

Using your mathematical skills, can you work out what comes next in each sequence?

103, 107, 109, 113, 127, ?

125, 61, 29, 13, 5, ?

2160, 360, 72, 18, 6, ?

30, 33, 66, 69, 138, ?

101, 99, 81, 72, 63, ?

Reasoning
KAKURO

This Japanese number crossword is also called Cross Sums.

Instructions

☐ Place a digit from 1 to 9 into each white square to solve the clues.

☐ Each horizontal run of white squares adds up to the total above the diagonal line to the left of the run, and each vertical run of white squares adds up to the total below the diagonal line above the run.

☐ No digit can be used more than once in any run.

Language
START AND END

For each line, can you find the missing letter that can be added to both the start and end to make a normal English word? For example, N could be added to _OO_ to make NOON.

NGAG

OTIO

_PA_

ACI

LPH

OIL

Total Brain Points

Reasoning
CORRAL

This logic puzzle involves building a fence around the given clues.

		3			6	4	
6					8		
		9	10			7	
2				7			
			5				5
	7			9	4		
		3					4
	8	3			3		

Instructions

☐ Draw a single loop along the grid lines such that each clue number can 'see' the given number of squares within the loop.

☐ The number of squares that a clue can see is the total count of interior squares in both horizontal and vertical directions from that square,
including the clue square itself (which is only counted once).

☐ The loop cannot cross or touch itself, even at a corner.

Re-Thinking

COMPRESSING MEMORY

Many of us find consciously learning facts quite difficult, and perhaps frustrating, but our brains are much better at it than we realize. Often just being reminded of something connected with what you're trying to remember is enough. That's why if you're trying to recall an event or something you intended to do, thinking about other things that happened at the same time will sometimes trigger the memory you wanted to recover.

Mnemonics are a great example of this. If you're trying to remember a set of facts, see if you can compress that information in some way, or associate it with something that's easier to remember. This works particularly well for sets and sequences, such as colours of the rainbow or the planets or whatever you need to remember. Taking the initials of a set of words, and making a single new word or phrase using those initials, can help – just learning that one new word or phrase will help you then retrieve all the other words by thinking about what the initials stood for.

Other techniques involve rhyming phrases, or witty ways of putting things that are interesting enough that you don't forget. At school you might have learnt the (not always helpful) phrase "I before E, except after C" – and because it rhymes, you never forgot it.

Instructions

☐ Next time you need to recall a set of facts, see if you can express them in a witty way that you can't forget.

☐ If you need to recall information in order, try using the initials of those words for a silly phrase. For example, to remember the biological order of taxonomy, Kingdom, Phylum, Class, Order, Family, Genus, Species, you can use "Kids Prefer Cheese Over Fried Green Spinach". Ridiculous, and therefore memorable.

Week 34 Solutions

Day 1

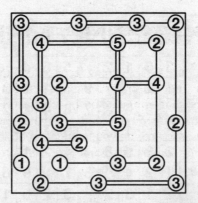

Day 2

Day 3

131: prime numbers in increasing order
1: subtract 3 and divide by 2 at each step
3: divide by 1 less at each step (6, 5, 4, 3, 2)
141: alternate between +3 and ×2 at each step
54: subtract the sum of the previous number's digits at
each step

Day 4

			8	18		12	31		
	4	16 17	7	9	16	7	9	7	
12	3	6	1	2	17 16	5	8	4	5
3	1	2	16 21	7	9	6 17	1	2	3
	15	9	6	22 11	7	8	4	1	2
	3	4 6	1	3	16 12	9	7	15	
22	2	3	5	8	4	3 12	2	1	7
7	1	2	4	15 3	8	7	15 3	9	6
	6	1	3	2	11	3	2	5	1
		3	2	1	3	2	1		

Day 5

ENGAGE
NOTION
SPAS
TACIT
ALPHA
SOILS

Day 6

		3			6	4	
6					8		
		9	10			7	
2				7			5
			5				5
	7			9	4		
		3					4
	8	3			3		

Week 35

Total Brain Points Available: **155**

Reasoning
DIAGONAL NUMBER LINK

This puzzle is considerably harder than regular Number Link!

1	2	3	1		4
		5		6	
				2	
6		5		4	3

Instructions

☐ Draw a series of separate paths, each connecting a pair of identical numbers, as in the example.

☐ No more than one line can pass through any square. They can only cross if they do so diagonally on the join between four squares.

☐ Lines can travel horizontally, vertically or diagonally between squares.

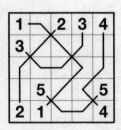

Language
LETTER SOUP

Rearrange these floating letters to spell out the names of five fruits. Each letter will be used in exactly one word.

Reasoning

LIGHTHOUSES

Can you locate all the ships in a stormy sea?

Instructions

□ Black squares with numbers on represent lighthouses. The number reveals how many ships can see that lighthouse. Ships can see a lighthouse if they are in the same row or column as the lighthouse.

□ Ships are one square in size, and cannot touch either each other or a lighthouse – not even diagonally.

□ Every ship can see at least one lighthouse.

Observation
MAZE

Find a path from the lighter circle (at the bottom) to the darker circle.

Language
LINK WORDS

Find a common English word to place in each gap, so that when attached to the end of the previous word or the start of the following word this makes two more English words. For example, BIRTH and BREAK could be linked with DAY, making BIRTHDAY and DAYBREAK.

HARD __ AGE

BUTTER __ BOARD

AIR __ ROPE

Reasoning
LINESWEEPER

This Minesweeper variant uses lines instead of mines!

			5						
								7	
	6				5	4			
	7								5
					5				
		8					7		
4				7		7			
		8						8	
		3		3		4			

Instructions

☐ Draw a single loop made up of horizontal and vertical lines.

☐ The loop can't cross or touch itself, and can only pass through empty grid squares.

☐ Squares with numbers indicate how many touching squares the loop passes through, including diagonally-touching squares.

Re-Thinking
WRITE IT DOWN

Writing things down can help in all kinds of ways. Firstly, it makes it harder to forget your thoughts, if you record them in a way you can later understand. Secondly, the act of being explicit about what you think can help force you to be clear about what you really do think. Thirdly, getting things out of your memory and onto paper can help free you to think up new thoughts without worrying about losing your concentration.

There are bound to have been times when you came across something you wanted to remember, and perhaps knew that you would never forget that thing – but that you then promptly forgot anyway. It happens to all of us, but there is an easy solution. Yes, it's called writing!

Don't just write, but draw diagrams too if appropriate. The more you can explain to yourself exactly what you're thinking and what you're planning to do, the more likely it is that you will have forced yourself to think things through properly – and the more likely it is that you'll think of the problems you initially missed!

Instructions

☐ Next time you come across something you want to remember, write it down. Just the act of writing something down can actually help you remember it, and you'll have a backup just in case you don't!

☐ If you can't express your idea or concept in relatively few words, or a simple diagram, the chances are you haven't really found the right solution or idea yet. Look for a concise summary of your thoughts, and write it down in a way anyone could understand.

Week 35 Solutions

Day 1

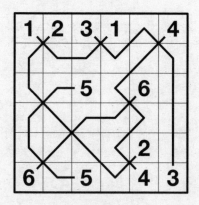

Day 2

GRAPEFRUIT

STRAWBERRY

MELON

PAPAYA

LEMON

Day 3

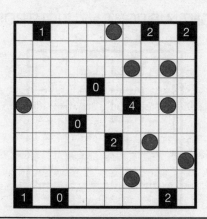

Date Completed

Week 35 Solutions

Day 4

Day 5

COVER: HARDCOVER and COVERAGE

CUP: BUTTERCUP and CUPBOARD

TIGHT: AIRTIGHT and TIGHTROPE

Day 6

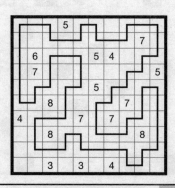

Week 36

Total Brain Points Available: **210**

Reasoning
TREN

This Japanese puzzle requires you to place blocks into a grid.

1			5				
					0		
	1			1			3
			0		2		
0		2			0		
	0					0	
				5			
0				2	0		

Instructions

- ☐ Draw 1x2 and 1x3 rectangular blocks along the grid lines such that each number is contained in exactly one block.
- ☐ The number in each block reveals the total count of squares the block can slide into. Vertical blocks slide in their columns; horizontal blocks slide in their rows.
- ☐ In the example, the '2' in the top row can slide up/down into two squares; the bottom row '1' can slide left/right into one square.

2		1		1
		2		
	1			
			1	1
	1			

Language
NEXT IN SEQUENCE

Can you work out what letter should come next in these two sequences? The sequences are made up of initials, so you need to work out what the initials stand for and then find the initial of the item that comes next.

For example, M T W T F would be followed by S, for Monday, Tuesday, Wednesday, Thursday, Friday and then Saturday.

F S T F F

H H L B B

Number Skills

FLOATING NUMBERS

For an extra challenge, try solving this entirely in your head!

34   **40**

33   **32**

26   **37**

23

Instructions

☐ Can you work out which of the floating numbers above you can add together to make each of the following totals?

☐ You can't use a floating number more than once in any given total.

81   **111**   **131**

Observation
REARRANGEMENT

This puzzle is a tricky test of your visual imagination skills.

Instructions

- ☐ Using just your imagination, work out which letter you would be able to form if you were to cut out and rearrange the positions of these six tiles.
- ☐ You can't rotate (or flip over/mirror image) any of the pieces – just imagine sliding them to new positions.
- ☐ This particular letter is using a stylized typewriter design, rather than a typical handwriting appearance.

Speed

WORD RECTANGLE

How many words can you find in this rectangle?

There are at least 30 to be found.

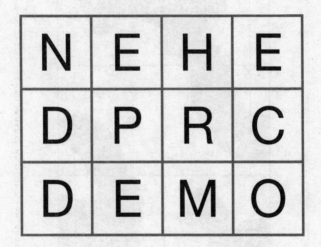

Instructions

- ☐ Make a word by starting on any letter and then tracing a path to adjacent letters, moving only to touching squares (including diagonally-touching squares).
- ☐ Every word must be at least three letters in length.
- ☐ The path can cross itself but it can't use any letter square more than once in a given word.
- ☐ There is a word that uses every square. Can you find it?
- ☐ Time yourself. How many words can you find in three minutes?

Total Brain Points

Reasoning
KROPKI

This puzzle combines a Latin Square with additional clues.

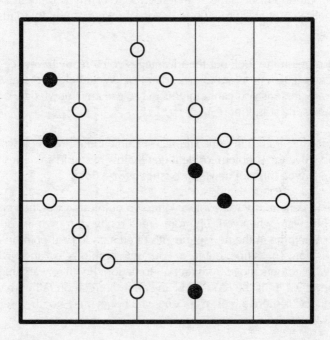

Instructions

☐ Place 1 to 5 once each into every row and column.
☐ Two squares with a black dot between contain numbers where one is twice the value of the other.
☐ Two squares with a white dot between contain consecutive numbers, such as 2 and 3, or 5 and 6.
☐ All possible black/white dots are given. If there is no dot, adjacent numbers are neither consecutive nor twice/half each other.
☐ Between 1 and 2 *either* a white or a black dot can be given.

Re-Thinking

MAKE YOURSELF THINK

Previous Re-Thinking topics have covered how explaining an idea, either out loud or on paper, can force you to clarify your ideas and will help you come across flaws in your thinking as you try to justify yourself.

It's also helpful to look out for advantages you already have. See if you can relate a problem to an earlier task. What helped there? Are there any lessons you can apply? Can I re-use any knowledge, or part of an existing solution?

Look for inspiration in unusual places. Think about how a clown would solve the problem, or deliberately invent stupid solutions – you may well think of new approaches as you do.

In life in general, try to develop your own opinions, or at the very least be aware when your opinions aren't really your own. If you read something in the newspaper, it's often a good deal opinion or supposition. That's fine, but form your own opinions too and try to spot when others move from fact on to fiction. If you're watching the news, when is the reporter giving an interpretation rather than a literal fact? Is there a bias, even one which they may not themselves be aware of?

Instructions

☐ Try not to accept everything you're told, or read. If someone tells you something, think about how they know it. If they can't possibly know it for certain, ask them why they believe it.

☐ It's very easy to be swayed by a negative viewpoint, and it's much easier to criticize than be constructive. Next time you come across a very negative viewpoint, see if you can work out for yourself whether the positives are being unfairly ignored. Don't forget that everyone has their own bias, whether they admit it or not.

Week 36 Solutions

Day 1

1			5				
					0		
	1			1			3
			0	2			
0		2			0		
	0					0	
				5			
0				2	0		

Day 2

S

Ordinal numbers in increasing order:
First Second Third Fourth Fifth Sixth

C

Chemical elements in increasing Periodic Table order:
Hydrogen Helium Lithium Beryllium Boron Carbon

Day 3

$$81 = 23 + 26 + 32$$

$$111 = 34 + 37 + 40$$

$$131 = 26 + 32 + 33 + 40$$

Week 36 Solutions

Day 4

Day 5

Possible words include:
CHROME, CHROMED, COME, COMP, COMPED,
COMPER, COMPREHEND, COMPREHENDED, COR,
CORE, CORED, CORM, CREPE, DEN, DEPEND, END,
ENDED, ERE, HEN, HER, HERE, HERO, MED, MERE,
MORE, OCHRE, ORE, PEN, PENDED, PER, PERCH,
PERCHED, PRO, PROM, RED, REDDEN, REND, REP,
ROC, ROMP, ROMPED

Day 6

1	4	3	5	2
2	1	4	3	5
4	5	1	2	3
3	2	5	1	4
5	3	2	4	1

Week 37

Total Brain Points Available: **205**

Reasoning

MASYU

This puzzle involves finding a loop through all of the circles.

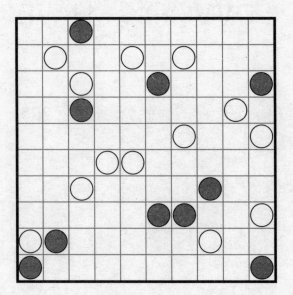

Instructions

☐ Draw a single loop that passes through the centre of every circle. Diagonal lines are not allowed.

☐ On a shaded circle the loop must turn 90 degrees and continue straight for at least one square on either side of the shaded circle.

☐ On a white circle the loop cannot turn, but it must then turn 90 degrees on either one or both of the adjacent squares.

☐ The loop cannot enter any square more than once.

Language
WORD CHAINS

Can you travel from the top to the bottom of these word chains?

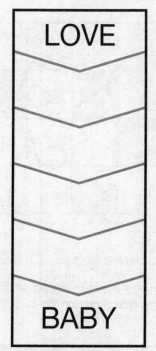

LOVE

BABY

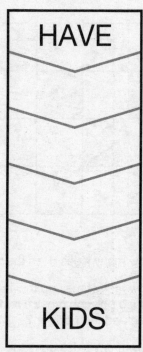

HAVE

KIDS

Instructions

- ☐ Fill in the empty steps with normal English words.
- ☐ At each step down the chain change just one letter to make a new word, but don't rearrange the other letters.
- ☐ There may be multiple ways to solve each chain, but you only need to find one solution per chain.

Observation
IMAGE COMBINATION

How good are you at combining images in your head?

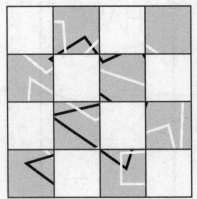 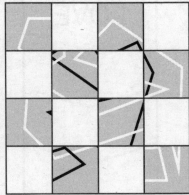

1. How many sides does the largest black-edged polygon have?

2. How many times do the lines that make up the largest white-edged polygon cross over the lines that make up the largest black-edged polygon?

3. How many sides does the smallest white-edged polygon have?

Instructions

☐ Imagine overlaying the two images above, so the gaps in one are filled with the content from the other.

☐ Answer the written questions, based on the combined image.

Sudoku

KILLER SUDOKU

Instructions

☐ Place 1 to 9 once each into every row, column and 3×3 box, while obeying the cage totals.
☐ The contents of each dashed line cage must sum to the total given at the top-left.
☐ You **cannot repeat a number** within a dashed line cage.

Speed

CRISS CROSS

How many of these words can you fit into the grid in three minutes?

3 Letters
Did
Inn
Urn

4 Letters
Aces
Spur
They
Wigs

5 Letters
Alpha
Merge
Poems
Tread

Exists
Magpie
Scenic
Weapon
Yields

6 Letters
Arisen
Banana
Damage

7 Letters
Cleaner
Gaining
Perhaps

Whistle

8 Letters
Insecure
Underlie

9 Letters
Education
Sincerely

Reasoning
FOUR WINDS

This logic puzzle is a good test of your spatial thinking.

Instructions

☐ Draw a horizontal or vertical line in every empty square, either passing through or stopping in that square.

☐ Lines must start at a black square.

☐ Numbers on black squares indicate the total number of white squares entered by lines starting at that square.

☐ Lines can only run horizontally and vertically and cannot bend.

☐ Lines can't cross, or touch more than one black square.

Re-Thinking
NOT BACKING DOWN

We all make mistakes from time to time, and sometimes we realize it. But how many of us will actually admit it?

Sometimes there are very good reasons for not admitting when you realize you're wrong, but in many cases it's merely pride that makes us stick to our story no matter what. Some people even have the ability to convince themselves that they really were correct, successfully suppressing their memory of being wrong.

We don't like to admit that we might not be perfect, so we come up with all kinds of reasons to explain what we said and what we did. Sometimes we are wrong, but because we really enjoy it when we're proven right about something we tend to remember the times we were right and forget the times we were wrong. Over time, this positive reinforcement of our own successes can lead some people to genuinely believe a version of their own past which is completely inaccurate, and hugely overestimate their own ability to be correct.

Bear in mind that other people are just like you – they tend to defend things they've said, even when they realize they're wrong, too. Try not to expect a perfection of others that you can't deliver yourself.

Instructions

☐ Next time you're involved in a disagreement with someone, take your time if you can. Stop to really think about what you're saying, and try to avoid the instinctive rush to prove why you were right. This rarely helps, because all parties end up being defensive.
☐ There is a lot of grey between definitely right and definitely wrong, and it can be useful to try to remember that! Sometimes things aren't as clear-cut as we think.

Week 37 Solutions

Day 1

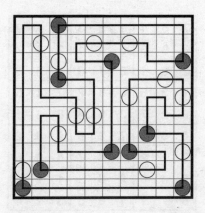

Day 2

LOVE
LORE
BORE
BARE
BABE
BABY

HAVE
HIVE
HIDE
RIDE
RIDS
KIDS

Day 3

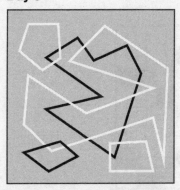

1) 8 sides

2) 6 times

3) 4 sides

Day 4

7	5	4	8	2	3	6	1	9
6	9	3	5	4	1	2	8	7
2	8	1	9	7	6	4	5	3
1	3	8	6	9	2	7	4	5
9	2	7	3	5	4	8	6	1
4	6	5	7	1	8	9	3	2
3	1	2	4	8	7	5	9	6
5	4	6	2	3	9	1	7	8
8	7	9	1	6	5	3	2	4

Day 5

MAGPIE   DAMAGE
 L   E D   I E   A
SPUR   UNDERLIE
 H   H C   G   N
BANANA   SCENIC
     P   T I   N
ACES   INN   WIGS
 L   O   C   H
WEAPON   EXISTS
 A   O   R   S   R
INSECURE   THEY
 E   M   R   L   L   A
ARISEN   YIELDS

Day 6

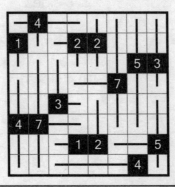

Week 38

Total Brain Points Available: **180**

Reasoning

HEYAWAKE

This Japanese logic puzzle's name translates as "Divided Rooms".

				0	3			
0								
					4			
		2						
5					4			
2					1			
2								

Instructions

- ☐ Shade some squares, such that no two shaded squares are adjacent, except diagonally, and all unshaded squares form a single continuous area.
- ☐ Any single horizontal or vertical line of unshaded squares cannot cross more than one bold line.
- ☐ Numbered squares may or may not be shaded, but always give the precise amount of shaded squares in their bold-lined region.

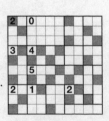

Total Brain Points

Language
MULTI-ANAGRAM

Can you find the given number of anagrams of each of the following sets of letters? Each anagram must be a standard English word, and it must use *all* of the given letters once each.

4 anagrams:
A E I N R R S T

3 anagrams:
D E E G I N R S

3 anagrams:
C G I N O R S U

Reasoning
BATTLESHIPS

Find the ships in this solo version of the classic two-player game.

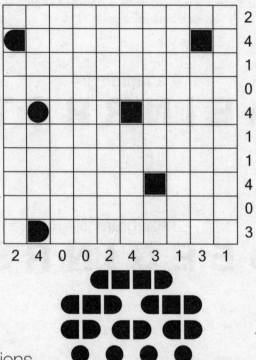

Instructions

- ☐ Locate the position of each of the listed ships in the grid. Ships are placed horizontally or vertically only.
- ☐ Numbers around the edge tell you the number of ship segments in each row and column.
- ☐ Ships can't touch each other, including diagonally.
- ☐ Some ship segments are already given.

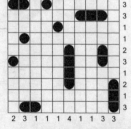

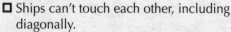

Total Brain Points

Observation
PHRASEOLOGY

This illustration represents a well-known phrase. Can you work out
what it is?

lucky

lucky ✕

lucky ✓

This second illustration also represents a well-known phrase. Can
you work out what phrase that is?

ANDCO
—
NQUER

Language
ARROWWORD

Solve this crossword where the clues are written inside the grid.

Plot outline ▼		Pool stick ▼		Knot ▼		Resistance unit
Sofa ▶				▼		Various
Whichever		Dutch-disease-prone trees ▶				▼
⌐▶			Cay		Plant with edible red root	
Relied upon		Unique book number (inits) ▶	▼		▼	
⌐▶						
Destitution		Sly look ▶				
⌐▶						

Reasoning
TOROIDAL NUMBER LINK

This puzzle allows lines to 'wrap around' from one side of the puzzle to the other!

			1	
2		3		
				1
		4	3	5
4			5	2

Instructions

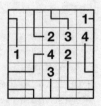

☐ Draw a series of separate paths, each connecting a pair of identical numbers, as in the example.

☐ No more than one line can pass through any square, and lines can only travel horizontally or vertically between squares.

☐ Paths are allowed to travel off the edge of the puzzle – if they do so then the same path continues at the opposite end of the same row or column.

Re-Thinking

CONSCIOUS THOUGHT

When you're speaking, how do you decide what to say? Do the words just come into your head as you speak?

Do you sometimes say something that you then find yourself defending? You explain why you said it, and you believe your explanation. But the truth is, often you are lying to yourself without even knowing it; in reality you really have no idea whatsoever why you said it – it just came out of your mouth, and then you instantly worked out why you thought you said it.

It may be a disconcerting idea, but if you think about it it's true. We are only consciously aware of a small amount of what goes on in our brains, and sometimes the unconscious part of our mind supplies the words. We do, from time to time, find ourselves saying something that even we ourselves know is stupid – and then we start justifying it, because saying that we don't know why we said it is clearly the first sign of madness. And yet, that's really how your brain works – and you're not mad! It's a team effort between the conscious and unconscious mind, and particularly if you're distracted or reacting on instinct (when you're angry, for example) you will sometimes say or do something that you later realize was far from sensible.

Instructions

☐ Next time you say something that you realize wasn't the smartest choice of words, take the time to think about why you said it. Admitting that you don't really know is not a flaw, and trying to understand the difference between what you really think, and what you find yourself saying, can help you clarify your thoughts more generally. Don't believe everything you say!

Week 38 Solutions

Day 1

Day 2

RESTRAIN STRAINER TERRAINS TRAINERS

DESIGNER REDESIGN RESIGNED

COURSING SCOURING SOURCING

Day 3

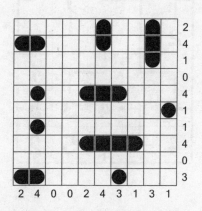

Day 4

Third time lucky

Divide and conquer

Day 5

Day 6

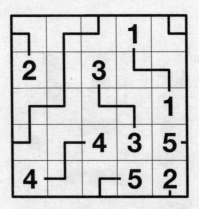

Week 39

Total Brain Points Available: **160**

Reasoning
FOUR-BRIDGE HASHI

This variant of the puzzle allows up to four bridges between islands.

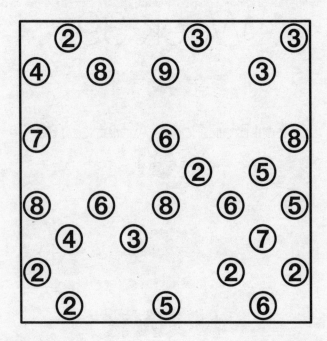

Instructions

☐ Join circled numbers with horizontal or vertical lines.

☐ Each number must have as many lines connected to it as specified by its value.

☐ No more than four lines may join any pair of numbers.

☐ No lines may cross.

☐ The finished layout must allow you to travel from any number to any other number just by following one or more lines.

Language
VOWEL PLAY

All of the vowels have been removed from the following words.
What were the original words? They are all common English words.

NMNT

FGL

CCL

NTWR

PQR

Number Skills
SCALES

Looking at the scales, can you say how much each shape weighs, in kilograms? Assume that every shape weighs the smallest possible number of whole kilograms it can. Ignore the distance from the fulcrum.

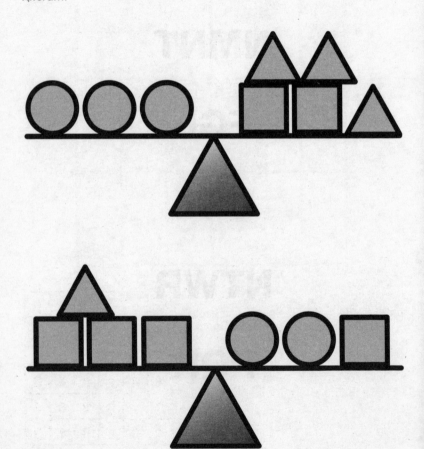

Reasoning
CALCUDOKU

This is another Latin Square puzzle, but this time the clues come in the form of mathematical constraints.

6×	2−	4×	48×	1−	
12×	5−	3+		6×	9+
		11+			
150×			2−	7+	3×
2÷					

Instructions

☐ Place the numbers 1 to 6 once each into every row and column of the grid, while obeying the region totals.

☐ The value at the top-left of each bold-lined region must be obtained when all of the numbers in that region have the given operation (+, -, ×, ÷) applied between them. For - and ÷ operations start with the largest number in the

6× 2	20× 5	4	24× 1	18× 3	6
3	4× 4	1	6	7+ 5	2÷ 2
90× 6	3	5	4	2	1
4− 1	6÷ 6	1− 2	12+ 3	4	5
5	1	3	4− 2	6	1− 4
6+ 4	2	6	5÷ 5	1	3

region and then subtract or divide by the other numbers.

Observation
CUBE COUNT

How many individual cubes have been used to build the structure below? You should assume that all 'hidden' cubes are present, and that it started off as a perfect 5×4×5 arrangement of cubes (right) before any cubes were removed. There are no floating cubes.

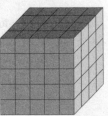

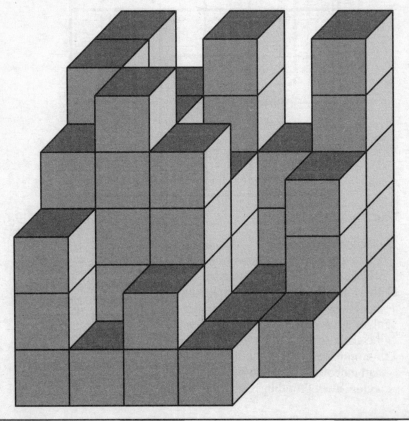

Reasoning
KUROMASU

This Japanese logic puzzle is a good test of your reasoning skills.

	9			7		4	
	4						
		2				6	
8							
	8				13		
		11				9	
							11
	13				17		
						11	
	10		7			3	

Instructions

☐ Shade in some squares, so that each number in the grid indicates the number of unshaded squares that can be seen from that square in the same row and column, including the square itself. Counting stops when you reach a shaded square.

☐ No square with a number in can be shaded.

☐ Shaded squares cannot touch, except diagonally.

☐ All unshaded squares must form a single continuous area, so you can move left/right/up/down from one unshaded square to another to reach any other unshaded square.

Re-Thinking

THE MOZART EFFECT

Some years ago it was widely reported that playing Mozart to children helped them do better at tests.

Unfortunately this turned out to be entirely misleading. Mozart does sometimes help, but so can anything that helps a child become relaxed and yet attentive before their exam. In fact, Mozart may not even be the best choice for the modern child!

Listening to Mozart won't make you noticeably smarter, or at least not if you listen to other music already – which nearly all of us do, whether through choice or not! But anything that puts you in a good mood and helps you feel relaxed can make you better prepared for a test of your mental powers.

Instructions

☐ Find some music you relax to, and listen to it next time you're feeling stressed before an important event.

☐ Try broadening your exposure to different types of music. This doesn't have to be music written before you were born, but if you're not familiar with much of it then why not start there? Start with Renaissance music (Byrd, Palestrina), then try Baroque music (J.S. Bach, Handel, Purcell), and then music of the Classical period (Beethoven, Mozart). Read about the harmony rules of each era.

Week 39 Solutions

Day 1

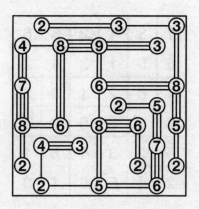

Day 2

NOMINATE

FUGAL

ICICLE

ANTIWAR

OPAQUER

Day 3

The triangle weighs 2kg

The square weighs 3kg

The circle weighs 4kg

Day 4

6× 1	2− 3	4× 4	48× 2	1− 5	6
6	5	1	3	4	2
12× 4	5− 6	3+ 2	1	6× 3	9+ 5
3	1	11+ 6	5	2	4
150× 5	2	3	2− 4	7+ 6	3× 1
2÷ 2	4	5	6	1	3

Day 5

Total cubes = 60

Counting the top layer as level 1, this is made up of:
Level 1 cubes = 5
Level 2 cubes = 9
Level 3 cubes = 13
Level 4 cubes = 14
Level 4 cubes = 19

Day 6

Week 40

Total Brain Points Available: **180**

Reasoning
MINESWEEPER

The classic game, as supplied with Windows™. This version can be solved using logic alone – no guessing is required!

	2						
2		2		2	3	3	
2		4	2				2
					2		1
			2		2		
	0				2	1	
	1				2		
		0			1	0	

Instructions

☐ Find the hidden mines in the grid.
☐ Mines can only be placed in empty grid squares.
☐ A number in a square reveals the number of touching mines, including diagonally.

●		1	1
●	4	2	●
●		●	3
1	3	●	

Language

CROSSWORD

Across

1 Disrupts (10)
5 Leaves of a book (5)
7 Premature (5)
9 Ensnarl (6)
10 Gravelly vocal sound (4)
12 Gap (4)
13 Place to see a film (6)
16 Sentient mammal (5)
17 Dance music (5)
18 Unofficially (10)

Down

1 Enter (5)
2 Outcome (6)
3 Addict (4)
4 Jeopardizes (9)
6 Adult male (9)
8 "Yeah" (3)
11 Insight (6)
12 'What's that?' (3)
14 Prolonged pain (5)
15 Aware of (4)

Number Skills
BRAIN CHAINS

Without using a calculator or making any written notes, solve each brain chain as quickly as you can.

| 80 | ×5 | -22% | +335 | -282 | -20% | RESULT |

| 215 | -20% | ÷2 | +383 | ×4/7 | -50% | RESULT |

| 328 | -211 | ×5/13 | -20% | -13 | ×6 | RESULT |

Instructions

☐ Start with the bold value on the left of the chain.
☐ Follow the arrow and apply the first operation. Remember the resulting value in your head.
☐ Follow the next arrow and apply the second operation to the value you remembered.
☐ Keep following arrows and applying operations until you reach the RESULT box. Write in the calculated value.

Speed
SPINNING LETTERS

How many words can you make from these letters in just five minutes?

There are around 100 to be found.

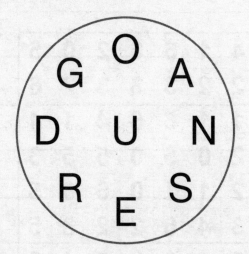

Instructions

☐ Make a word by using the middle letter plus any selection of the other letters, each used no more than once per word.

☐ Every word must be at least three letters in length, and must be a regular English word – proper nouns are not allowed.

☐ If you don't get anywhere near 100 words in five minutes, you can always give yourself as much extra time as you need.

Concentration
DOMINO SET

This game is not logically difficult but it requires concentration to solve, to keep track of your progress cleanly in order that you don't miss any "obvious" deductions.

	0	1	2	3	4	5	6
0							
1							
2							
3							
4							
5							
6							

4	4	1	6	6	2	0	5
4	2	2	3	3	3	2	6
0	1	1	6	6	4	1	4
0	2	0	5	0	5	5	3
4	2	1	1	0	6	0	5
1	3	4	6	2	2	3	5
5	3	1	6	3	5	4	0

Instructions

☐ Draw solid lines to divide the grid up to form a complete set of standard dominoes, with one of each domino.

☐ A '0' represents a blank on a traditional domino.

☐ Use the check-off list to help you keep track of which dominoes you've placed.

6	0	0	4	2	1	5	4
3	5	2	6	0	4	2	1
2	5	3	2	0	1	4	4
1	6	0	2	0	1	2	1
1	3	3	5	3	5	5	3
6	6	6	6	2	0	6	4
1	0	4	5	3	3	5	4

Reasoning
FENCE POSTS

This brain challenge uses only basic reasoning tricks, but can still be tricky to solve!

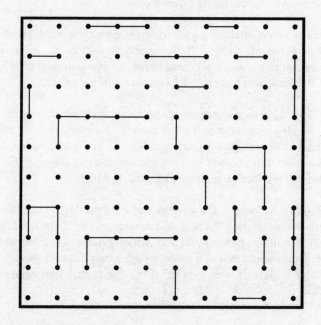

Instructions

- ☐ Join all of the dots to form a single loop.
- ☐ The loop cannot cross or touch itself at any point.
- ☐ Only horizontal and vertical lines between dots are allowed.
- ☐ Some parts of the loop are already given.

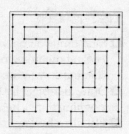

Re-Thinking
SPATIAL AWARENESS

We all live in a 3D world, and have a basic ability to walk or cycle or drive from A to B without bumping into things. It's lucky, really, else we'd have trouble going anywhere!

Particularly when driving quickly, or crossing a busy road, good spatial awareness is a key skill. Being able to rapidly transform a map into expectations about upcoming bends, or see potential problems before they become too close to avoid, can prove critical.

When driving, using your mirrors effectively makes you a much safer driver – both for yourself and other drivers. But many people still have trouble translating left and right between mirrors and reality – do you ever find yourself looking for the steering wheel in the reflection to work out which side of a car is which?

It's a good idea, then, to think about these things when your life isn't hanging in the balance. As odd as it may sound, practise looking in the mirror at things behind you and working out where they really are relative to you. Look at a map or GPS when out and about (preferably walking!), and then see if the reality matched what you expected.

Instructions

- ☐ Next time you pack a suitcase or a lunchbox or some such, think about how you fit the objects in together. What is the most efficient way to use the space available?
- ☐ Draw an object by looking at its reflection in the mirror. Practise touching things behind you using only the mirror.
- ☐ Visualize folding paper before actually trying it. Can you predict what shape each fold, or series of folds, will result in?

Week 40 Solutions

Day 1

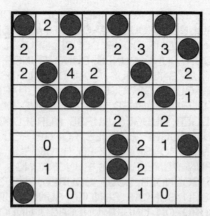

Day 2

I	N	T	E	R	R	U	P	T	S
N			E		S		H		
P	A	G	E	S		E	A	R	L	Y
U		E		U		R		E		E
T	A	N	G	L	E		R	A	S	P
		T		T		W		T		
H	O	L	E		C	I	N	E	M	A
U		E		O		S		N		G
H	U	M	A	N		D	I	S	C	O
		A		T		O				N
	I	N	F	O	R	M	A	L	L	Y

Day 3

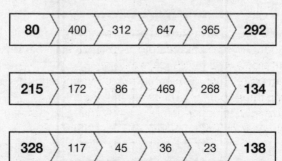

| 80 | 400 | 312 | 647 | 365 | 292 |

| 215 | 172 | 86 | 469 | 268 | 134 |

| 328 | 117 | 45 | 36 | 23 | 138 |

Week 40 Solutions

Day 4

Possible words include: AGROUND, AGUE, ARGUE, ARGUED, ARGUES, AROUND, AROUSE, AROUSED, ASUNDER, AUGER, AUGERS, DANGEROUS, DOUR, DOUSE, DRUG, DRUGS, DUE, DUES, DUG, DUN, DUNE, DUNES, DUNG, DUNGS, DUO, EURO, EUROS, GENUS, GNU, GNUS, GOURD, GOURDS, GROUND, GROUNDS, GROUSE, GROUSED, GUANO, GUARD, GUARDS, GUN, GUNS, GURN, GURNED, GURNS, NOUS, NUDE, NUDES, NUDGE, NUDGER, NUDGES, NURSE, NURSED, ONUS, OUR, OURS, RESOUND, ROGUE, ROGUES, ROUGE, ROUGED, ROUGES, ROUND, ROUNDS, ROUSE, ROUSED, RUDE, RUE, RUED, RUES, RUG, RUGS, RUN, RUNE, RUNES, RUNG, RUNGS, RUNS, RUSE, SNUG, SOUND, SOUNDER, SOUR, SOURED, SUE, SUED, SUGAR, SUGARED, SUN, SUNDAE, SUNDER, SUNG, SURE, SURGE, SURGED, SURGEON, UNDER, UNDERGO, UNDO, UNDOES, UNREAD, URGE, URGED, URGES, URN, URNS, USAGE, USE, USED, USER

Day 5

4	4	1	6	6	2	0	5
4	2	2	3	3	3	2	6
0	1	1	6	6	4	1	4
0	2	0	5	0	5	5	3
4	2	1	1	0	6	0	5
1	3	4	6	2	2	3	5
5	3	1	6	3	5	4	0

Day 6

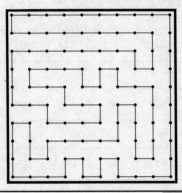

Current Brain Rank

Week 41

Total Brain Points Available: **175**

Reasoning
FUTOSHIKI

These puzzles combine inequalities with Latin Squares.

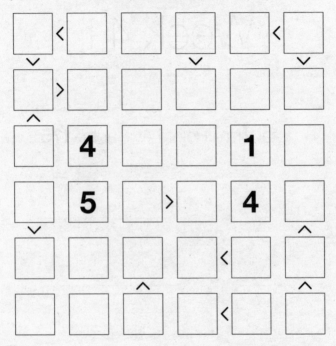

Instructions

☐ Place 1 to 6 once each into every row and column while obeying the inequality signs.

☐ Less than ("<") and greater than (">") signs between some squares indicate that the values in these two squares must be greater than or less than one another as indicated by the sign. The sign always points towards the smaller number.

Language
WORD PYRAMID

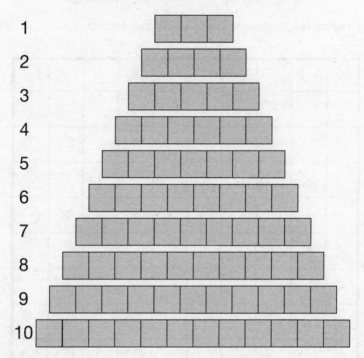

1. Farmyard animal
2. The microwave's ready?
3. Mimicking
4. Growing whiter
5. A young tree
6. Satisfactory
7. Falling back into old habits
8. Rendering
9. Spilling paint?
10. Very loud

Instructions

☐ Each row of bricks uses the same letters as the row above it except for the addition of one extra letter. The letters may be rearranged, however, so KIT can be on the row above TICK.

☐ Solve the clues to help you fill the pyramid.

Concentration
NO 4 IN A ROW

This puzzle is a tougher, solo version of noughts and crosses.

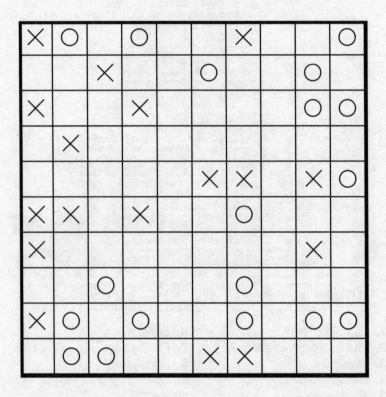

Instructions

☐ Fill the empty squares in the grid with either an 'X' or an 'O'
such that no line of four consecutive 'X's or 'O's is made in any
direction, including diagonally.

Observation

MATCHING PAIRS

Instructions

☐ A set of objects have been split in two, and the various resulting half-objects are shown above.

☐ Can you pair each object with its other half?

Speed

WORDSEARCH

How many of the listed websites can you find in this grid within three minutes? They can be written in any direction, either forwards or backwards.

Popular Websites

A	O	W	A	E	E	G	M	L	D	G	E	B	A	Y
E	L	B	I	T	O	I	Y	S	I	N	O	G	M	O
V	B	B	T	S	E	R	E	T	N	I	P	A	A	K
I	R	K	C	I	L	F	O	P	O	B	I	T	Z	D
L	O	O	O	L	E	P	W	O	L	N	E	O	O	M
S	Y	M	Y	S	S	E	O	O	H	A	Y	P	N	M
W	S	G	T	G	O	O	G	L	E	O	G	I	P	T
O	O	S	O	I	I	G	G	S	U	C	D	L	S	L
D	I	L	E	A	E	B	O	T	T	E	B	E	E	U
N	B	B	Z	R	S	C	U	I	K	V	N	N	C	M
I	A	I	D	C	P	B	M	N	I	I	F	N	F	U
W	I	K	I	P	E	D	I	A	M	K	B	D	O	O
T	D	T	U	M	B	L	R	E	T	T	I	W	T	K
E	U	F	A	C	E	B	O	O	K	R	A	O	F	E
U	A	E	M	G	W	M	L	L	W	E	S	E	P	G

AMAZON	FACEBOOK	TUMBLR
BAIDU	FLICKR	TWITTER
BING	GOOGLE	WIKIPEDIA
BLOGGER	IMDB	WINDOWS LIVE
BLOGSPOT	LINKEDIN	WORDPRESS
CRAIGSLIST	MSN	YAHOO
EBAY	PINTEREST	YOUTUBE

Reasoning
LIGHT UP

This Japanese logic puzzle is also known as 'Akari'.

Instructions

- ☐ Place light bulbs in white squares so that all of the white squares either contain a bulb or are lit by at least one bulb.
- ☐ Light bulbs illuminate all squares in the same row and column up to the first black square encountered in each direction.
- ☐ No light bulb may illuminate any other light bulb.
- ☐ Black squares with numbers indicate how many light bulbs are placed in the touching squares (above/below/left/right).
- ☐ Not all light bulbs are necessarily clued.

Re-Thinking
DON'T STULTIFY

Do you have a routine? How fixed is it? Is there much variation in it, or can you predict fairly accurately in advance what you'll be doing at any given time on any day in the future?

Routines can be an important part of managing your daily life, and in many ways they are desirable. But like all things in life, they can be taken to extremes. It's important to ensure that you don't convert your life into a series of tasks that you end up executing in an automatic, robot-like fashion. Try to keep things fresh, in whatever way you can. If you're not having to consciously think about a task, your brain isn't learning anything new.

At the most basic level, see if you can rearrange parts of your routine. Maybe keep the same elements but change the order, or if you are able to then try swapping an existing activity for something slightly different.

Take a new route when you drive to a regular destination, or if you read a newspaper then buy a different one at least once in a while. It's good to keep your mind fresh, and to change your viewpoint – both literally and figuratively.

Instructions

- ☐ Is there some routine part of your life that you do on auto-pilot? Try changing some aspect of it a little in order to make you think, even if this means you need to allow a few extra minutes for it.
- ☐ Pretend for a minute that you don't know anything about yourself! Try watching some TV you think you won't enjoy, or reading a book you "know" you'll hate, or listening to a music artist you wouldn't normally try. At worst, you'll feel you've wasted a bit of time or money. At best, you'll discover something new you enjoy.

Week 41 Solutions

Day 1

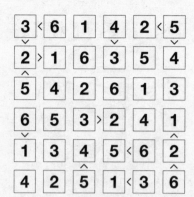

Day 2

PIG
PING
APING
PALING
SAPLING
PLEASING
RELAPSING
PLASTERING
SPLATTERING
EARSPLITTING

Day 3

X	O	X	O	O	X	X	X	O	O
O	X	X	X	O	O	O	X	O	X
X	O	O	X	X	O	X	O	O	O
X	X	X	O	O	O	X	O	X	O
O	O	O	X	O	X	X	O	X	O
X	X	O	X	X	X	O	X	O	X
X	X	X	O	O	O	X	X	X	O
O	O	O	X	X	O	O	O	X	O
X	O	X	O	O	X	O	X	O	O
X	O	O	X	O	X	X	X	O	X

Week 41 Solutions

Day 4

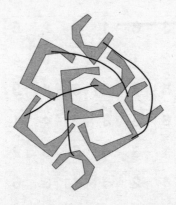

Day 5

Day 6

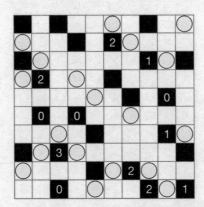

Week 42

Total Brain Points Available: **140**

Reasoning

YAJILIN

This Japanese logic puzzle combines route-finding with logical deductions based on the given clues.

(Grid puzzle with clues: 3↓, 2↑, 2↑, 1↓, 0←, 5↑)

Instructions

☐ Draw a single loop using only horizontal and vertical lines such that the loop does not pass through any square more than once.

☐ Any squares which the loop does not visit must be shaded, but none of these shaded squares can touch in either a horizontal or vertical direction.

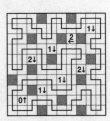

☐ Numbers with arrows indicate the exact number of shaded squares in a given direction in a specific row or column, but not all shaded squares are necessarily identified with arrows.

Total Brain Points

Language

DELETED PAIRS

How quickly can you identify each of these concealed words?

DT ER MA NO PS TI RT AI TO EN

AP BL UE MN DT EI NF TU SL

SG TA EL LA LC AT RI EC

EI DN IT TE OL OL RE EC ST

Instructions

☐ Delete one letter from each pair so that each line spells out a
   word. For example: D̶E F̶O G̶J to spell out **DOG**.

Number Skills
NUMBER PATH

Fill in the empty squares in this grid to reveal a hidden path.

52									9
	50							15	
		35			18				
	41					20			
	66				91				
		68			83				
	71							98	
75									100

Instructions

☐ Fill empty squares so that the completed grid contains every number from 1 to 100 exactly once each.

☐ Place the numbers so that there is a route from 1 to 100 that visits every grid square exactly once each in increasing numerical order, moving only left, right, up or down between touching squares.

Observation
JIGSAW CUT

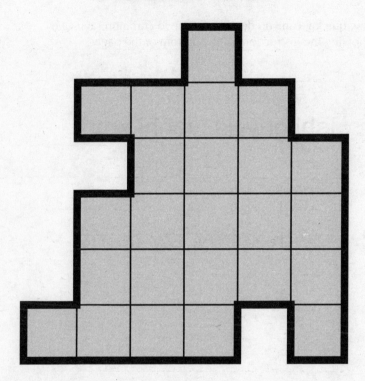

Instructions

- ☐ Draw along the existing lines to divide this shape up into four identical jigsaw pieces, with no pieces left over.
- ☐ The pieces may be rotated versions of one another, but you cannot mirror or 'turn over' any of the pieces.

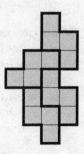

Speed

CRYPTOGRAM

How quickly can you decode these two common sayings by following the instructions at the bottom of the page?

1. Tshj gnyyjs, ybnhj xmd

2. Tzy tk xnlmy, tzy tk rnsi

Instructions

☐ Both phrases have been encrypted using the same code.
☐ Each letter has been replaced with another letter a fixed number of places forward/backward in the alphabet, wrapping around from Z to A. The number of places shifted is the same for all letters. For example, A might be replaced with C; B replaced with D; C replaced with E; and so on, until X is replaced with Z; Y is replaced with A; and Z is replaced with B.

Total Brain Points

Reasoning
RECTANGLES

This Japanese logic puzzle is also known as Shikaku.

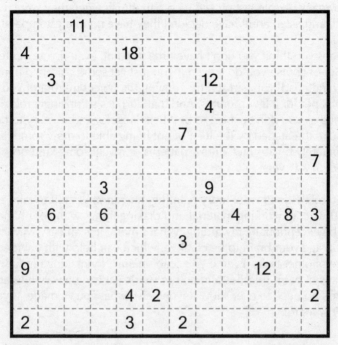

Instructions

☐ Draw solid lines along some of the dashed lines in order to divide the grid up into a set of rectangles, such that every number is inside exactly one rectangle.

☐ The number inside each rectangle must be exactly equal to the number of grid squares that the rectangle contains, so a '4' could be in a 2×2 or a 4×1 (or 1×4) rectangle.

☐ All grid squares are used.

Re-Thinking

ART

You might like nothing better than putting paint on canvas, but a great many people last picked up a paintbrush when they were a child, and as an adult have decided they have no interest in painting.

Perhaps you think you don't have time to paint, even if you wanted to. But of course you do – even if you just get some coloured pencils and a notepad, you can still try copying the object in front of you onto paper for a few minutes. And that's art. It's surprisingly relaxing, so long as you don't expect to be Michelangelo, and it's easy to do. If you're threatened by the idea of not being able to draw something, deliberately be abstract – draw patterns or invent some kind of "modern art" version.

If you really don't want to try painting, find another craft to take up. The act of working material and making things with your hands can be exceptionally rewarding. What's more, it is an easy way to encourage your brain to be creative, which can help with a wide range of other tasks. Even if you "can't paint", try making random designs of paint splashes and colour swirls – it can be very liberating. There's no need to ever show anyone else what you've made, if you don't want to!

Instructions

☐ Get some paints and brushes, even if that's a kid's pack of watercolours. If you're looking for inspiration, make a watery red or orange and paint across the paper, then repeat with a watery yellow above and a watery blue above that. Congratulations, you've created a sunset using a wash technique! Let the watery paints mix to produce various colour effects. And once it's dry, use black paint to paint silhouettes on. Now you have a finished night-time scene!

Week 42 Solutions

Day 1

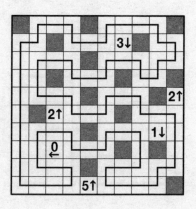

Day 2

TRANSITION
PLENTIFUL
GALACTIC
INTELLECT

Day 3

52	51	38	37	32	31	12	11	10	9
53	50	39	36	33	30	13	14	15	8
54	49	40	35	34	29	18	17	16	7
55	48	41	42	43	28	19	20	5	6
56	47	46	45	44	27	22	21	4	3
57	60	61	62	63	26	23	92	93	2
58	59	66	65	64	25	24	91	94	1
73	72	67	68	81	82	83	90	95	96
74	71	70	69	80	85	84	89	98	97
75	76	77	78	79	86	87	88	99	100

Week 42 Solutions

Day 4

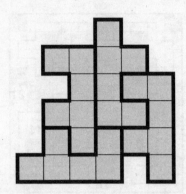

Day 5

Decode each of these quotations by replacing A with V, B with W, C with X and so on through to replacing Y with T and Z with U

Once bitten, twice shy

Out of sight, out of mind

Day 6

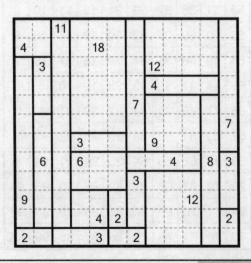

Week 43

Total Brain Points Available: **170**

Reasoning
NUMBER LINK

This route-finding puzzle requires a mix of reasoning and observation skills.

							1	2	
	3					3	4		
							1		
		5							
	6		4	7			8		
					8	9			5
10				6			2	11	
	12	10						13	
		14				7			
		15				9			
	12							13	11
			15			14			

Instructions

- ☐ Draw a series of separate paths, each connecting a pair of identical numbers, as in the example.
- ☐ No more than one line can pass through any square, and lines can only travel horizontally or vertically between squares.

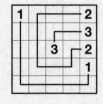

Language
ANAGRAMS

Find an anagram of the CAPITALIZED word in each sentence that can go in the gap.

1. We _____ with the DROLLEST comedian.

2. He had a HEARTIER, _____ type of wit.

3. They searched around the _____ with FORENSIC detail.

4. The man has to _____ as he CLAMBERS over the obstructions.

5. The vegetables need IMMERSING in the _____ solution.

6. The nurse needs to _____ the BACTERIAL count.

Concentration
BINARY PUZZLE

Fill the empty grid squares with 0s and 1s to make a series of binary numbers.

		1					
	0		1	0		1	
		0				1	0
			1	0			
		1	1			1	
0	0					0	
				1	0		

Instructions

☐ Place a 0 or 1 in every empty square so that there are four of each in every row and column.

☐ Reading across or down a row or column, there may be no more than two of the same digit in succession.

Sudoku

SUDOKU

See how quickly you can solve this classic number placement puzzle.

		6				3		
	2		1		8		9	
1		3				4		2
	9			7			3	
		4		2				
	6			9			8	
3		7				9		6
	1		6		7		2	
		2				8		

Instructions

☐ Place 1 to 9 exactly once each in every row, column and bold-lined 3×3 box.

Speed

LETTER ORBITS

How many English words can you find? There are about 35 in total.

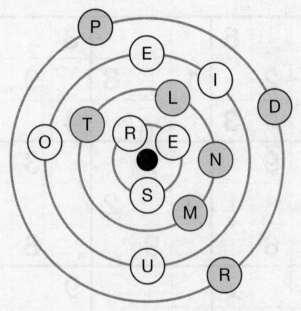

Instructions

☐ By picking one letter from the outermost orbit, then one letter from each orbit in turn through to the innermost orbit, how many four-letter English words can you find?

☐ The letters must remain in the order of the orbits, with the outermost orbit's letter first and so on.

☐ Time yourself. How many words can you find in three minutes?

Total Brain Points

Reasoning
SKYSCRAPER

In this puzzle a number inside the grid represents a skyscraper of that many floors. So a '3' is a three-storey building, while a '5' is a five-storey building. Taller buildings obscure shorter ones.

```
        4       2
  3  ┌───┬───┬───┬───┬───┐
     │   │   │   │   │   │
     ├───┼───┼───┼───┼───┤
     │   │   │   │   │   │
     ├───┼───┼───┼───┼───┤
  4  │   │   │   │   │   │
     ├───┼───┼───┼───┼───┤
     │   │   │   │   │   │
     ├───┼───┼───┼───┼───┤
  3  │   │   │   │   │   │
     └───┴───┴───┴───┴───┘
        3       2
```

Instructions

☐ Place 1 to 5 once each into every row and column of the grid.

☐ Place buildings in the grid in such a way that each given clue number *outside* the grid represents the number of buildings that can be seen from that point, looking only at that clue's row or column.

	2	4			
2	5	3	4	1	
5	4	1	3	2	4
1	3	5	2	4	
3	2	4	1	5	
4	1	2	5	3	
	2	5		1	

☐ A building with a higher value always obscures a building with a lower value, while a building with a lower value never obscures a building with a higher value.

Re-Thinking
ARTWORKS

Last week's Re-Thinking talked about making your own art, but it's also good to go and see other people's art. It takes a while to read a book or watch a film, but a painting can give you a pretty instantaneous impression of how someone else sees the world, and that can be pretty interesting for your brain.

Many people are put off art galleries and the like because they think they don't know enough about art to really enjoy it. But the fact of the matter is, most people have no idea who painted virtually any painting, or made any given sculpture, just as most people can't tell you whether they're listening to Mozart or Bach. That doesn't mean you can't enjoy art, of whatever form it is. In fact, you'll have a purer and less biased perception of the art, and so should get a more genuine reaction to the exhibit.

If you look at a painting and you understand something of what the painter was trying to communicate, then art is working for you. If you look at it and you have no clue what they were aiming for, maybe they've failed. If the explanation next to it tells you it's about saving the planet and it's a picture of a table, chances are the artist didn't really know what it was about either. It's better to worry about the people who apparently "get it" than the fact that you don't yourself!

Instructions

☐ Visit an art gallery, if you can, or look at the paintings in public or civic buildings.

☐ Think about which pictures you find particularly interesting, and see if you can work out what they are supposed to be about.

☐ Don't worry about what other people think of art. Your perception is deeply personal, and no one else is likely to think and feel exactly the same as you. There's no right or wrong in art.

Week 43 Solutions

Day 1

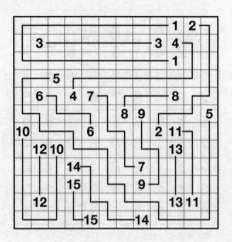

Day 2

STROLLED
EARTHIER
CONIFERS
SCRAMBLE
SIMMERING
CALIBRATE

Day 3

0	0	1	0	1	1	0	1
0	0	1	1	0	1	1	0
1	1	0	0	1	0	1	0
0	1	0	1	0	1	0	1
1	0	1	1	0	0	1	0
0	0	1	0	1	0	1	1
1	1	0	1	0	1	0	0
1	1	0	0	1	0	0	1

Week 43 Solutions

Day 4

9	7	6	5	2	4	3	1	8
4	2	5	1	3	8	6	9	7
1	8	3	7	6	9	4	5	2
2	9	4	8	7	6	1	3	5
5	3	8	4	1	2	7	6	9
7	6	1	3	9	5	2	8	4
3	5	7	2	8	1	9	4	6
8	1	9	6	4	7	5	2	3
6	4	2	9	5	3	8	7	1

Day 5

Possible words include:
DENS, DIME, DIMS, DINE, DINS, DOLE, DOME, DONE, DONS, DOTE, DOTS, DUNE, DUNS, PENS, PETS, PILE, PINE, PINS, PITS, POLE, POLS, POTS, PUNS, PUTS, REMS, RILE, RIME, RIMS, RITE, ROLE, ROTE, ROTS, RULE, RUMS, RUNE, RUNS, RUTS

Day 6

		4		2	
3	**3**	4	1	5	2
	4	5	3	2	1
4	2	3	4	1	5
	5	1	2	4	3
3	**1**	2	5	3	4
		3		2	

Week 44

Total Brain Points Available: **155**

Reasoning
SLITHERLINK

Just draw a loop, in this incredibly pure logic puzzle.

```
  3     3     3     2 2
2                 3     1 3
  3     1 2     2     3
3   0     3
1           2         2     2
2     2       1           3
              3     2     3
    0     2     2 3     2
  3 1   2                 3
    2 2     2     1     3
```

Instructions

- Draw a single loop by connecting together the dots so that each numbered square has the specified number of adjacent line segments.
- Dots can only be joined by straight horizontal or vertical lines.
- The loop cannot touch, cross or overlap itself in any way.

```
  2   2   2 2
    2 1 2     1 3
3     1 1     1     2
  3 1   2 1 1
    2 2 2   3 2
2     2     0 1     2
2 3     0 1 1
    2 1   3   2
```

Language
CODEWORD

Work out the number-to-letter substitution code to create a regular filled crossword grid, which uses only standard English words.

A	21	2 **A**	12	9		8	2	7	7		N
B	13		20		13	12	16		13		2	O
C	6	16	3	15	13		14 **D**	13	9	16	1	P
D	16		23		18		1		23		23	Q
E	10	11	11	18		9	13	24	2	19	13	R
F	5				14		14				13	S
G	5				14		14				13	T
H	12	3	11	22 **K**	13	17		18	4	10	12	U
I	13		3		26		4		23		13	V
J	11	2	10	19	13		2	21	10	13	11	W
K	15		18		20	3	18		18		15	X
L		11	13	25	15		5	3	15	18		Y
M		11	13	25	15		5	3	15	18		Z

1	2	3	4	5	6	7	8	9	10	11	12	13
14	15	16	17	18	19	20	21	22	23	24	25	26

Number Skills

NUMBER DARTS

Can you hit the given totals on this number dartboard?

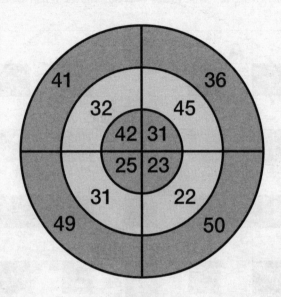

99   107   118

Instructions

☐ By choosing exactly one number from each ring of this dartboard, can you find three numbers whose values add up to the first listed total? Now repeat with the other two totals.

☐ For example, you could form 88 with 41 + 22 + 25.

Observation
SUBDIVISION

This puzzle will test your spatial reasoning.

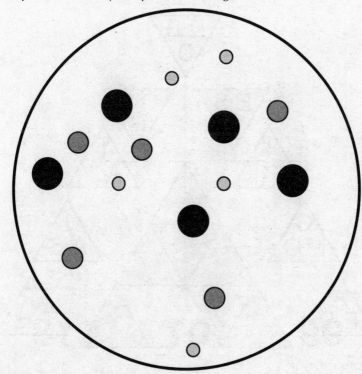

Instructions

☐ Draw four straight lines in order to divide this circle up into exactly five areas.

☐ Each area must contain one of each size of shaded circle.

☐ The lines you draw should start at one edge of the circle, and not cross any other line you draw. They may end either at another edge of the circle or when they reach another line.

Language
LETTER TRIANGLES

Can you fit all the letter jigsaw pieces to spell out one word per row?

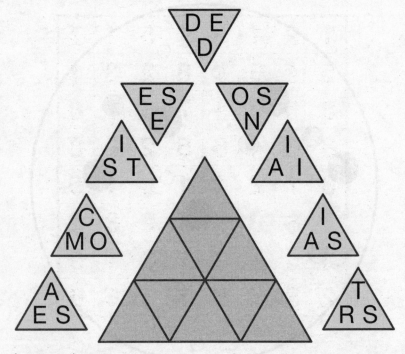

Instructions

☐ Place the triangular jigsaw pieces into the empty pyramid in order to spell out a word reading across each row. There are therefore six words to be found.

☐ Each piece is used only once and may not be rotated or reflected – place them in exactly the same orientation as they are given.

Reasoning
HITORI

This puzzle is in some respects like Sudoku in reverse!

1	2	1	6	1	5	1	7
5	4	6	2	8	2	3	1
3	5	2	1	7	4	7	8
8	6	4	6	5	2	2	3
3	7	2	4	1	6	1	5
7	8	3	8	4	2	8	2
6	3	1	7	1	8	1	5
2	8	7	8	3	1	5	6

Instructions

☐ Shade in squares so that no number occurs more than once per row or column.

☐ Shaded squares cannot touch in either a horizontal or vertical direction.

☐ All unshaded squares must form a single continuous area, so you can move left/right/ up/down from one unshaded square to another to reach any unshaded square.

2	7	8	8	6	8	3	3
5	1	6	1	2	3	4	2
7	6	2	8	5	4	8	3
3	2	4	5	4	7	6	8
8	5	5	8	7	4	2	3
3	8	3	4	2	5	7	1
4	5	3	7	8	2	1	3
1	3	1	2	1	6	7	4

Re-Thinking
REGRETS

It's usually better to regret trying something than *not* having tried. At least in the former case you'll know that you gave it a go, whereas in the latter you'll just never know. It's good to have the satisfaction of at least knowing for certain what happened when you did try!

As you get older, it's natural to collect regrets. Most of us have them, but what's important is to not let them control you. Regrets are useful only in so much as they improve our behaviour in the future – by reminding us of things we've learnt, or perhaps by reminding us to give something a go next time we have the chance!

When regret isn't helpful is when it leads to paralysis, or becomes excessively negative. You need to live in the now, because the past is gone and in the most literal sense is never coming back. Many people have regrets connected with relationships at some point, but it's important not to beat yourself up for a long time over your perceived mistakes. It's easy to focus on a decision or two and blame them for something that went wrong, but the truth is usually far more complex than you realize. Worse still, over time you forget the other details and remember only the regret. When you find yourself doing this, you need to try to let go.

Instructions

☐ You can't control everything you think about, and we all have quiet moments. But when you find yourself focusing too much attention on something you really have no control over, try to realize that it's a waste of your time that would be better spent on something else.

☐ Turn regrets into life lessons. Shift your focus from the negative to the positive, and see them as a growth and learning experience, no matter how painful they were at the time.

Week 44 Solutions

Day 1

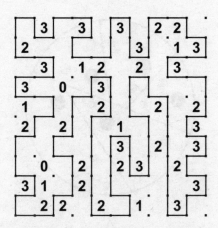

Day 2

Day 3

$$99 = 36 + 32 + 31$$

$$107 = 50 + 32 + 25$$

$$118 = 50 + 45 + 23$$

Week 44 Solutions

Day 4

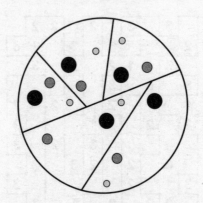

Day 5

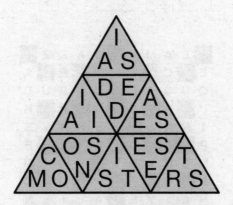

Day 6

1	2	1	6	1	5	1	7
5	4	6	2	8	2	3	1
3	5	2	1	7	4	7	8
8	6	4	6	5	2	2	3
3	7	2	4	1	6	1	5
7	8	3	8	4	2	8	2
6	3	1	7	1	8	1	5
2	8	7	8	3	1	5	6

Week 45

Total Brain Points Available: **185**

Reasoning
HANJIE

This popular picture-revealing puzzle is published under a range of names, including Griddler™, Nonogram and Pic-a-pix.

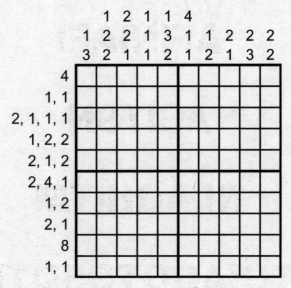

Picture clue: Quack!

Instructions

☐ Shade in squares in the grid to reveal a picture by obeying the clue constraints at the start of each row or column.

☐ The clues provide, in order, the length of every run of consecutive shaded squares in their row or column.

☐ There must be a gap of at least one empty square between each run of shaded squares in the same row or column.

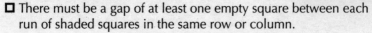

Language
WORD SEQUENCES

Can you work out the well-known sayings represented by each set of initials?

AFINIAFI

ASITSN

NLAGHITM

TGIAGOTOSOTF

WIRDATRD

FRIWAFTT

Concentration
KING'S JOURNEY

Fill the grid squares to reveal a hidden path, which can include diagonal moves.

	10					16	17
	7	9		14		19	
		46				52	
2		44	43		49		21
1							22
	64	35	37	40			55
		36		39	27		24
	61						

Instructions

☐ Fill empty squares so that the completed grid contains every number from 1 to 64 exactly once each.
☐ Place the numbers so that there is a route from 1 to 64 that visits every grid square exactly once each in numerical order, moving only left, right, up, down or diagonally between touching squares.

Observation
CIRCUIT BOARD

Which piece fits in the gap?

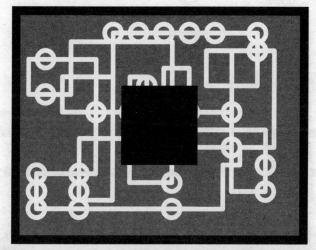

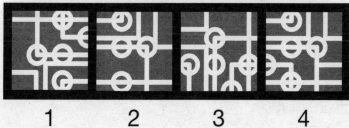

1   2   3   4

Instructions

☐ Can you work out which one of the four pieces fits into the gap, in order to complete the circuit board? Once complete all of the lines will connect at both ends.

☐ You may need to rotate the correct piece.

Speed

WORD SLIDER

Imagine you've cut out each of these columns of letters, plus the central window.

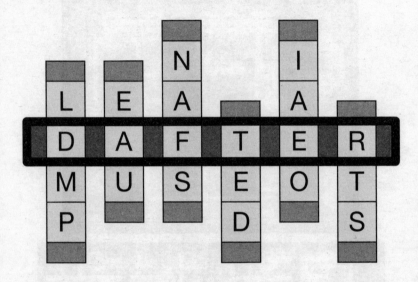

Instructions

- ☐ By imagining moving each of the sliders up and down, you can reveal different letters and read words through the central window.
- ☐ Each word must use a letter from every slider – you can't slide them out of the window. Therefore each word will be six letters long.
- ☐ One word is spelled out for you already. Can you find 20 further English words in just three minutes?

Reasoning
ARROWS

One of the keys to being able to solve this puzzle is working out a good way of making notes, so you can keep track of your deductions.

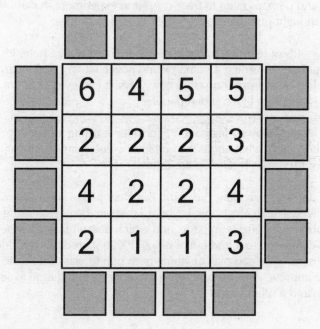

Instructions

☐ Place an arrow into every box outside the grid. Each arrow can point up, down, left, right or in one of the four principle diagonal directions.

☐ Every arrow must point to at least one number.

☐ When correctly placed, the numbers in the grid must be equal to the count of the number of arrows that are pointing at that number.

Re-Thinking
BE A MUSICIAN

Learning to play an instrument gets you thinking in all kinds of new ways. You will learn to focus on a tune, to hear harmonies in new ways, and perhaps even to free yourself to experiment in ways you never thought possible. You're never too old to start!

The benefits of learning to make music are hard to overstate. It's great for your brain, learning a complex and novel activity, and it can help you relax, or express yourself in new ways. It can even help connect you socially with like-minded people.

If you already play an instrument, consider learning a new one. If you play piano, what about the guitar, or vice-versa? Or pick up a flute, or trumpet. Or take up the drums!

If you don't already play, the piano is a great pick – you can buy a relatively cheap electronic keyboard that can be played using headphones if noise is an issue, and which doesn't take up much space compared to a traditional piano. It's an incredibly versatile instrument – you can play anything from pop to classical music, and as you improve you can progress from a one-fingered tune to simple chords and a fuller sound.

Instructions

☐ Is there an instrument you like the sound of, or think it would be fun to play? A simple acoustic guitar won't cost you much at all, but it can take a month before your fingers stop hurting from the strings, so if you can afford a cheap electronic keyboard that's a great place to begin. And unlike most instruments, every time you hit a key you'll get a perfect note! It takes practice to get a clean note from a wind or stringed instrument.

Score   Total Brain Points

Week 45 Solutions

Day 1

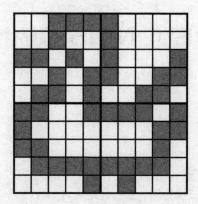

Day 2

A friend in need is a friend indeed
A stitch in time saves nine
Never look a gift horse in the mouth
The grass is always greener on the other side of the
fence
When in Rome, do as the Romans do
Fools rush in where angels fear to tread

Day 3

6	10	11	12	13	15	16	17
5	7	9	47	14	51	19	18
4	8	46	45	48	50	52	20
2	3	44	43	42	49	53	21
1	32	31	30	29	41	54	22
33	64	35	37	40	28	23	55
63	34	36	38	39	27	56	24
62	61	60	59	58	57	26	25

Week 45 Solutions

Day 4

Circuit piece 3

Day 5

Possible words include:
DAFTER, DEADER, DEFEAT, DEFTER, DUSTER,
LANDER, LEADER, LENDER, LUSTER, MANDIR,
MANTAS, MANTIS, MASTER, MENDER, MENTOR,
MUFTIS, MUSTER, PANDAS, PANDER, PANDIT,
PANTOS, PASEOS, PASTAS, PASTER, PASTES,
PASTIS, PASTOR, PESTER, PESTOS, PUNDIT,
PUNTER

Day 6

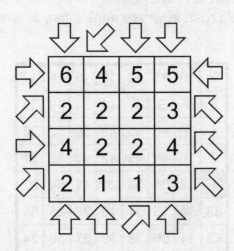

Week 46

Total Brain Points Available: **140**

Reasoning
EASY AS ABC

Place A, B and C in every row and column, using the external clues.

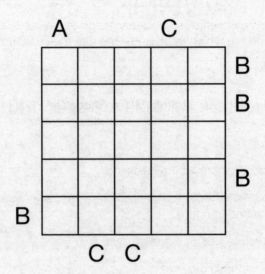

Instructions

☐ Fit the letters A, B and C exactly once each into every row and column of squares inside the empty grid. Two squares in each row or column will therefore be empty.

☐ Letters outside the grid indicate which letter appears closest to that end of the row or column.

Total Brain Points

Language
COMPREHENSION

Read the following series of statements, then fill out the empty table at the bottom of the page appropriately.

Three friends each enjoyed a sugary snack this week. Can you work out who ate which treat, and what day they consumed it?

Names: Dan, Matt, Sara
Confectionery items: Toffee, Mints, Chocolate
Days: Tuesday, Thursday, Saturday

1. Sara had her snack at the weekend.

2. The mints-eater enjoyed their treat two days after the toffee was consumed.

3. The chocolate wasn't eaten on Tuesday.

4. Dan did not have the mints.

Name	Confectionery	Day

Number Skills

NUMBER PYRAMID

Complete this number pyramid using just addition and subtraction.

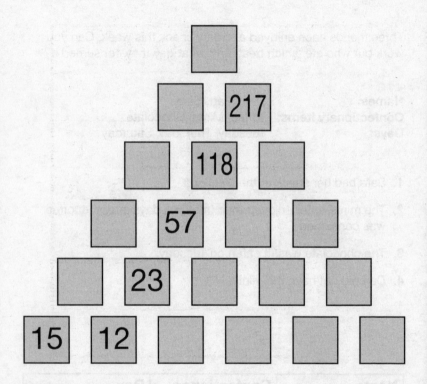

Instructions

☐ Fill in empty bricks so that each brick contains a value equal to the sum of the two bricks directly beneath it.

Score   Total Brain Points

Sudoku
JIGSAW 7×7

This jigsaw twist on Sudoku ramps up the difficulty level more than you might expect!

	B			D	G	
						F
E	C				D	A
G						
	D	E			B	

Instructions

☐ Place 1 to 7 once each into every row, column and bold-lined jigsaw region.

Score   Total Brain Points   **465**

Language
WORD FRAGMENTS

Rearrange the fragments on each line to make a complete word.

NF AT ER ED NS IO CO

ON IC TI FL IN

LY AST RT HE ER NO

G EN IN AR DE

RS M TE ES SE

OU TF LY GH UL TH

Score | Total Brain Points

Reasoning
NURIKABE

This Japanese logic puzzle is sometimes called Islands in the Stream.

		5					1
			6				
							1
8							
							4
6							
							3
2							
					3		
5						2	

Instructions

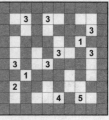

- ☐ Shade in squares so that every number in the puzzle remains as part of a continuous unshaded area of precisely the given number of squares.
- ☐ There can be only one number per unshaded area.
- ☐ Shaded squares cannot form any solid 2×2 (or larger) areas.
- ☐ All the shaded squares must form one continuous area.

Re-Thinking
SOLVING PROBLEMS

Various techniques for getting going on tricky problems have been discussed in previous Re-Thinkings, but there is a range of further techniques which can help in some cases.

One such technique is trying to put yourself in someone else's shoes. See if you can work out what they would do, if they had the same problem. Think about their particular view on the world. These need not seem especially practical. For example, what would a superhero do? What would a cartoon character do? It may or may not help, but it's worth giving it a go when you need inspiration!

Think about a prominent government figure, or a celebrity. If they were in this situation, what do you think they'd do?

Sometimes it's easier to picture other people solving a problem because it helps separate off any personal anxiety you might feel. It also – just like explaining a problem out loud – helps trigger different parts of your clever brain, and it can help it follow thinking paths that you'd perhaps unwittingly shut off when trying to solve the problem as yourself.

Instructions

☐ Try building yourself a toolkit of characters to help solve your problems. Maybe pick a favourite superhero, cartoon character, politician and celebrity. Then next time you're stuck, see what they'd do!

☐ Still stuck? Have them form a team and work together on the project!

☐ It's best not to include in a formal report that Scooby Doo, Jennifer Aniston, Teddy Roosevelt and Superman helped you out.

Week 46 Solutions

Day 1

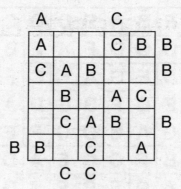

Day 2

Sara - Chocolate - Saturday
Dan - Toffee - Tuesday
Matt - Mints - Thursday

Day 3

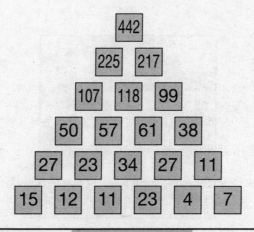

Week 46 Solutions

Day 4

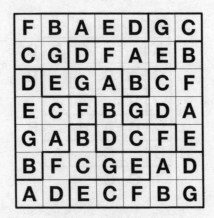

F	B	A	E	D	G	C
C	G	D	F	A	E	B
D	E	G	A	B	C	F
E	C	F	B	G	D	A
G	A	B	D	C	F	E
B	F	C	G	E	A	D
A	D	E	C	F	B	G

Day 5

CONFEDERATIONS
INFLICTION
NORTHEASTERLY
ENDEARING
SEMESTERS
THOUGHTFULLY

Day 6

Week 47

Total Brain Points Available: **235**

Reasoning
HASHI

The full Japanese name of this puzzle is Hashiwokakero, but it is often also known as Bridges.

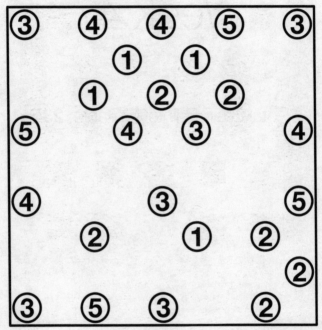

Instructions

☐ Join circled numbers with horizontal or vertical lines.

☐ Each number must have as many lines connected to it as specified by its value.

☐ No more than two lines may join any pair of numbers.

☐ No lines may cross.

☐ The finished layout must allow you to travel from any number to any other number just by following one or more lines.

Language

CRYPTIC CROSSWORD

Across

3 Great card! (3)
6 Faithful previous scene (5)
7 As I'd say under my breath (5)
8 Associate surrounded by marsh grass was not forgotten (10)
14 Penny-pinching git returns odd hat (5)
15 Criticize and scrutinize TV movie edit? (3,3,4)
21 Choose to behead the elite (5)
22 Communists hold article studies (5)
23 Notice odd kitchen strainer (3)

Down

1 Find out hospital has organ (4)
2 Ham sandwiches rule is an abuse (4)
3 A cat is very small (4)
4 Help hear vowels (4)
5 Function from uneasiness (4)
9 Kit out in fit of pique (5)
10 River 'X' was consumed (5)
11 Legume with good centre got rolling (5)
12 Look intently - all crazy charges! (5)
13 Pet's mother, maybe, has settled view (5)
16 Games company turns itself around but still grows old (4)
17 Performs Luke's sequel (4)
18 Be brave and gargle a red (4)
19 Chlorine added to pre-noon mollusc (4)
20 Finds messy den (4)

Number Skills

NUMBER SEQUENCES

Using your mathematical skills, can you work out what comes next in each sequence?

1.16666, 1.2, 1.25, 1.33333, 1.5, ?

2, 3, 5, 8, 13, 21, ?

4096, 1024, 256, 64, 16, ?

197, 193, 191, 181, 179, ?

5, 8, 12, 18, 24, 30, ?

Reasoning
KAKURO

This Japanese number crossword is also called Cross Sums.

Instructions

- ☐ Place a digit from 1 to 9 into each white square to solve the clues.
- ☐ Each horizontal run of white squares adds up to the total above the diagonal line to the left of the run, and each vertical run of white squares adds up to the total below the diagonal line above the run.
- ☐ No digit can be used more than once in any run.

Language
START AND END

For each line, can you find the missing letter that can be added to both the start and end to make an English word? For example, N could be added to _OO_ to make NOON. The last one on this page is more obscure than the others.

IBE

UPP

NATHEM

_AI_

_UR_

PHELI

Reasoning
CORRAL

This logic puzzle involves building a fence around the given clues.

		7			10	7	
2			5	5			
				6			
5					6		5
5		4					4
			4				
			8	8			6
	3	4			3		

Instructions

☐ Draw a single loop along the grid lines such that each clue number can 'see' the given number of squares within the loop.

☐ The number of squares that a clue can see is the total count of interior squares in both horizontal and vertical directions from that square, including the clue square itself (which is only counted once).

☐ The loop cannot cross or touch itself, even at a corner.

Re-Thinking
PUZZLE SELECTION

It's tempting to skip puzzles that we find challenging, whether in life or in the relatively unimportant confines of this book, and yet the chances are that those are the puzzles from which our brains will gain the most mental benefit.

Next time you're stuck on a puzzle, stop and realize that perhaps this means that this is the puzzle you really should look at. Of course, if instead the problem is that the puzzle is too easy for you, the chances are that you'll get little mental benefit from it and so feel free to skip it!

Continually challenging yourself is the key aim of this book. The puzzles do vary in difficulty but within each puzzle type there is a progression from easier at the start towards harder at the end. There are exactly four of each type of puzzle in the book, and in all cases the easier ones appear first and the harder ones appear last. However, if you find otherwise, that's actually a good thing – once you solve a few puzzles of a type, if you come to a harder one and then find it easier, that's fantastic! It's likely that you're demonstrating an improvement in your abilities, at least on that type of puzzle!

Instructions

- ❑ There are 78 different types of puzzle in this book, and by this point you should have completed three or four of each type.
- ❑ Are there any puzzles you've skipped in earlier weeks? Go back and try them again – do you find them easier now? If not, try to take the time to learn to solve these puzzles, perhaps using some of the techniques discussed earlier in the book. Remember that guessing is a perfectly legitimate solving method, at least to help you get started on a puzzle and tease out how the logic works! Guessing is never required for the puzzles in this book, however.

Week 47 Solutions

Day 1

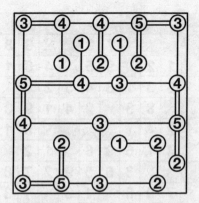

Day 2

Day 3

2: sequence is 7/6, 6/5, 5/4, 4/3, 3/2, 2/1

34: sum the previous two numbers

4: divide by 4 at each step

173: prime numbers in decreasing order

36: sum of the first and second primes (2+3), then the sum of the second and third primes (3+5), then the sum of the third and fourth primes (5+7), and so on

Week 47 Solutions

Day 4

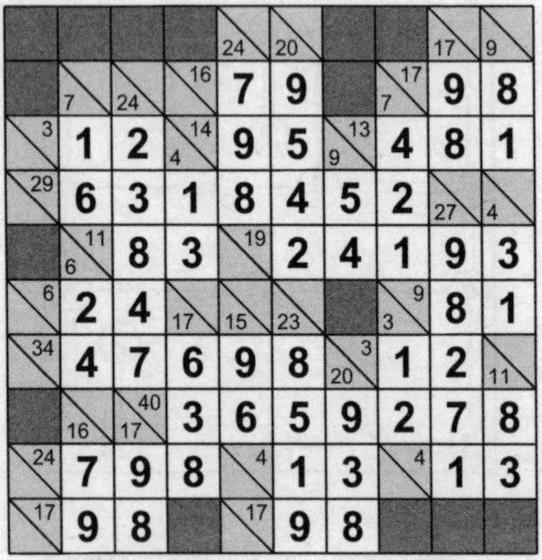

Day 5

LIBEL
YUPPY
ANATHEMA
MAIM
AURA
APHELIA

Day 6

Week 48

Total Brain Points Available: **155**

Reasoning
DIAGONAL NUMBER LINK

This puzzle is considerably harder than regular Number Link!

1		2			3
4					
	5				4
	3				6
					5
6	1				2

Instructions

- ☐ Draw a series of separate paths, each connecting a pair of identical numbers, as in the example.
- ☐ No more than one line can pass through any square. They can only cross if they do so diagonally on the join between four squares.
- ☐ Lines can travel horizontally, vertically or diagonally between squares.

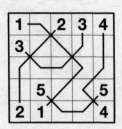

Language
LETTER SOUP

Rearrange these floating letters to spell out the names of five vegetables. Each letter will be used in exactly one word.

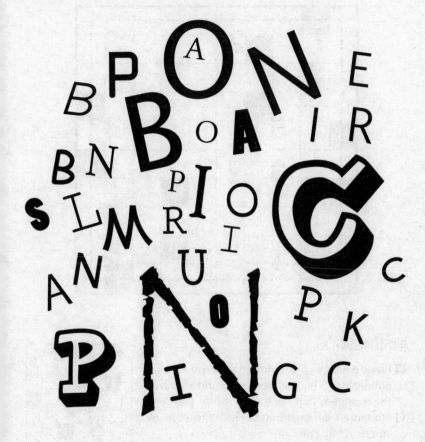

Reasoning
LIGHTHOUSES

Can you locate all the ships in a stormy sea?

	2								
			3						
			1						0
0									
									2
0						1			
						2			
								1	

Instructions

☐ Black squares with numbers on represent lighthouses. The number reveals how many ships can see that lighthouse. Ships can see a lighthouse if they are in the same row or column as the lighthouse.

☐ Ships are one square in size, and cannot touch either each other or a lighthouse – not even diagonally.

☐ Every ship can see at least one lighthouse.

Observation
MAZE

Find a path from the lighter circle (at the bottom-left) to the darker circle.

Language
LINK WORDS

Find a common English word to place in each gap, so that when attached to the end of the previous word or the start of the following word this makes two more English words. For example, BIRTH and BREAK could be linked with DAY, making BIRTHDAY and DAYBREAK.

DOG ___ MAN

BROAD ___ AWAY

CAR ___ WIDE

Reasoning
LINESWEEPER

This Minesweeper variant uses lines instead of mines!

			5						3
		3		6				5	
							5		
	6			6			7		
			3						
		6						7	
4					7				
		7	7						
									3

Instructions

- ☐ Draw a single loop made up of horizontal and vertical lines.
- ☐ The loop can't cross or touch itself, and can only pass through empty grid squares.
- ☐ Squares with numbers indicate how many touching squares the loop passes through, including diagonally-touching squares.

Re-Thinking

SLEEPING ON THE JOB

Previous Re-Thinking pages have discussed how important sleep is to all aspects of your brain.

Sleep doesn't just need to be overnight. Some cultures routinely take naps during the day, and it does seem to be natural to have a second period of rest during mid-afternoon, or the corresponding time during whatever hours you're awake. So it's actually okay to have a two-hour rest and then sleep two hours less later on. Just try to make sure that your total sleep adds up to what you need, which is often said to be at least seven hours on average.

Winston Churchill famously slept for only around four hours a night, but he also took a two-hour sleep in the afternoon. Of course, if you're going to take sleep outside night-time then you need to be sure it's actual sleep, without people disturbing you. And while you can split your sleep into two sessions, going beyond that won't work for most people.

If you regularly have trouble sleeping, you should consult an expert who can help you sort it out – a lack of sleep will lead to a whole host of issues, and it is very bad news for your brain.

Instructions

☐ Many people have no ability to take a nap during the afternoon, due to working in an office or having responsibilities they can't avoid. But if you have the option to take an hour or two's break, you could try it. See how it works for you. Of course, many of us also need to fit in with other people's schedules, so if you end up staying up late and disturbing others then maybe this isn't such a good idea! But it's important to remember that there's nothing wrong with a second period of sleep during the day.

Week 48 Solutions

Day 1

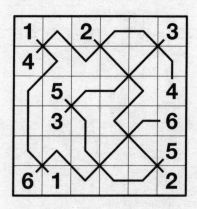

Day 2

CABBAGE

BROCCOLI

ONION

PUMPKIN

PARSNIP

Day 3

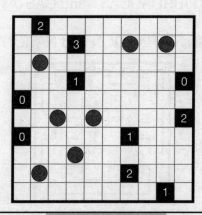

Week 48 Solutions

Day 4

Day 5

WOODS: DOGWOODS and WOODSMAN
or HOUSE: DOGHOUSE and HOUSEMAN
or WATCH: DOGWATCH and WATCHMAN

CAST: BROADCAST and CASTAWAY

NATION: CARNATION and NATIONWIDE

Day 6

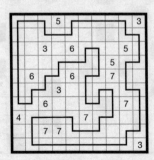

Week 49

Total Brain Points Available: **220**

Reasoning
TREN

This Japanese puzzle requires you to place blocks into a grid.

				2	1		
							1
				5			
		5		0			
3						5	0
			4				
	1		3				
			4				1

Instructions

- ☐ Draw 1x2 and 1x3 rectangular blocks along the grid lines such that each number is contained in exactly one block.
- ☐ The number in each block reveals the total count of squares the block can slide into. Vertical blocks slide in their columns; horizontal blocks slide in their rows.
- ☐ In the example, the '2' in the top row can slide up/down into two squares; the bottom row '1' can slide left/right into one square.

Language
NEXT IN SEQUENCE

Can you work out what letter should come next in these two sequences? The sequences may be either initials or some other sequence of single letter identifiers.

For example, M T W T F would be followed by S, for Monday, Tuesday, Wednesday, Thursday, Friday and then Saturday.

C G D A E

P C O F G

Number Skills
FLOATING NUMBERS

For an extra challenge, try solving this entirely in your head!

40   **38**

20   **41**

27 **44**

32

Instructions

☐ Can you work out which of the floating numbers above you can add together to make each of the following totals?

☐ You can't use a floating number more than once in any given total.

100   150   175

Observation
REARRANGEMENT

This puzzle is a great test of your visual imagination skills.

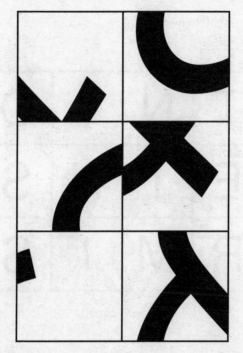

Instructions

- ☐ Using just your imagination, work out which keyboard symbol you would be able to form if you were to cut out and rearrange the positions of these six tiles.
- ☐ You can't rotate (or flip over/mirror image) any of the pieces – just imagine sliding them to new positions.

Speed
WORD RECTANGLE

How many words can you find in this rectangle?

There are at least 50 to be found.

T	N	I	O
E	I	N	S
R	M	I	S

Instructions

☐ Make a word by starting on any letter and then tracing a path to adjacent letters, moving only to touching squares (including diagonally-touching squares).

☐ Every word must be at least three letters in length.

☐ The path can cross itself but it can't use any letter square more than once in a given word.

☐ There is a word that uses every square. Can you find it?

☐ Time yourself. How many words can you find in four minutes?

Reasoning
KROPKI

This puzzle combines a Latin Square with additional clues.

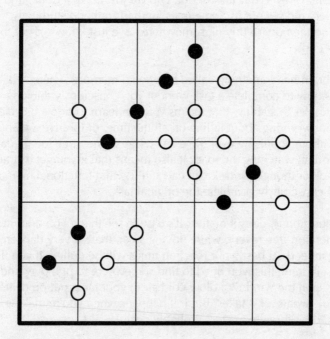

Instructions

- ☐ Place 1 to 5 once each into every row and column.
- ☐ Two squares with a black dot between contain numbers where one is twice the value of the other.
- ☐ Two squares with a white dot between contain consecutive numbers, such as 2 and 3, or 5 and 6.
- ☐ All possible black/white dots are given. If there is no dot, adjacent numbers are neither consecutive nor twice/half each other.
- ☐ Between 1 and 2 *either* a white or a black dot can be given.

5	3	1	2	4
3	5	4	1	2
2	4	5	3	1
1	2	3	4	5
4	1	2	5	3

Re-Thinking
AUTOPILOT

We've all done it. We can't remember whether we've completed an ordinary, everyday task or not. Did we just make a drink, and if so where did we put it? Sometimes, perhaps rather disturbingly, we have no memory of driving somewhere – we just know we got there in the end!

Your brain has something called functional memory, whereby it learns how to complete a task without you consciously thinking about it. It's this ability that means you can learn to ride a bicycle without worrying about falling off all the time, or to drive a manual car without agonising over the exact usage of the three foot pedals rather than watching the road. It also means that if you get distracted by another thought or task you can still use that functional memory to subconsciously complete the original task.

The question is, does it matter? It's easy to see that if you drift into an attention-free reverie while driving a car, that's a very dangerous thing indeed. At best, your reaction times will be dulled. If you find yourself doing this, you need to find somewhere to pull over and rest. Open the windows; blow cold air in your face; put on deafening music – whatever it takes. But if it happens when you're making a drink, does it really matter? Probably not.

Instructions

☐ Next time you find yourself wondering whether you have done something, try saying what you're doing aloud to yourself in future. Just the act of vocalizing your intentions will help you remember what you're doing and have done. This can also work more generally for remembering things.

☐ If something is so mundane that you don't remember it, maybe it's time for a change! Take a different route when driving, or start having a different drink. Change your routine in some way.

Week 49 Solutions

Day 1

Day 2

B

Major scales in increasing number of sharps:

C G D A E B

S

Biological classifications in increasing specificity:

Phylum Class Order Family Genus Species

Day 3

$$100 = 27 + 32 + 41$$

$$150 = 27 + 38 + 41 + 44$$

$$175 = 20 + 32 + 38 + 41 + 44$$

Day 4

Day 5

Possible words include:
EMIR, EMISSION, EMIT, INN, INNER, INNS, INS,
INTER, INTERIM, INTERMISSION, ION, IONS, IRE,
ITEM, MEN, MERINO, MERINOS, MERIT, MET, MIEN,
MINE, MINER, MINI, MINION, MINIONS, MINIS, MINT,
MINTER, MIRE, MISS, MISSION, MITE, MITER, NET,
NINE, NIT, REIN, REINS, REMISS, REMISSION, REMIT,
RENT, RIM, RIME, RITE, SIN, SINE, SINNER, SINS,
SIS, SON, SONNET, SONS, TEN, TENNIS, TERM,
TERMINI, TIE, TIER, TIME, TIMER, TIN, TINE, TINS,
TIRE

Day 6

3	5	2	4	1
1	2	4	3	5
5	1	3	2	4
2	4	5	1	3
4	3	1	5	2

Week 50

Total Brain Points Available: **205**

Reasoning
MASYU

This puzzle involves finding a loop through all of the circles.

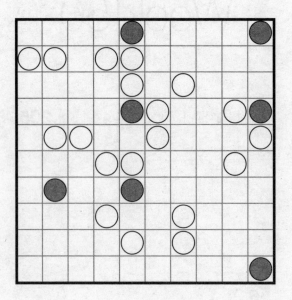

Instructions

☐ Draw a single loop that passes through the centre of every circle. Diagonal lines are not allowed.

☐ On a shaded circle the loop must turn 90 degrees and continue straight for at least one square on either side of the shaded circle.

☐ On a white circle the loop cannot turn, but it must then turn 90 degrees on either one or both of the adjacent squares.

☐ The loop cannot enter any square more than once.

Language
WORD CHAINS

Can you travel from the top to the bottom of these word chains?

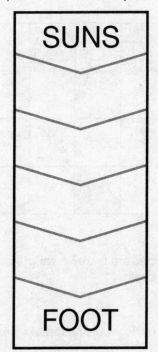

SUNS

FOOT

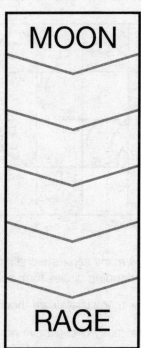

MOON

RAGE

Instructions

- ☐ Fill in the empty steps with normal English words.
- ☐ At each step down the chain change just one letter to make a new word, but don't rearrange the other letters.
- ☐ There may be multiple ways to solve each chain, but you only need to find one solution per chain.

Observation
IMAGE COMBINATION

How good are you at combining images in your head?

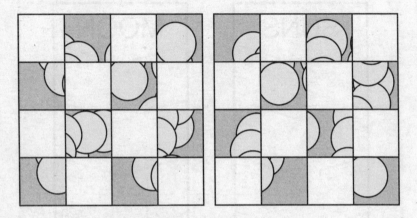

1. How many separate chains of circles are there? A set of overlapping circles form a single chain.

2. How many circles are there in total?

3. How many circles have no other circle visibly on top of them?

Instructions

☐ Imagine overlaying the two images above, so the gaps in one are filled with the content from the other.

☐ Answer the written questions, based on the combined image.

Sudoku

KILLER SUDOKU

Instructions

- ☐ Place 1 to 9 once each into every row, column and 3×3 box, while obeying the cage totals.
- ☐ The contents of each dashed line cage must sum to the total given at the top-left.
- ☐ You **cannot repeat a number** within a dashed line cage.

Speed

CRISS CROSS

How many of these words can you fit into the grid in three minutes?

3 Letters
Act
Amp
Bar
Eta
Ifs
Lap
Orb
Ups

4 Letters
Anti
Dark
Prey
Rake
Stir
Trap

5 Letters
Allow
Bushy

Cobra
Mimic
Odium
Pasha
Plume
Strip
Timer
Typed

6 Letters
Artful
Cuckoo
Extent
Gateau
Helium
Hiring
Threat
Tunnel
Tuxedo
Update

Reasoning
FOUR WINDS

This logic puzzle is a good test of your spatial thinking.

Instructions

- ☐ Draw a horizontal or vertical line in every empty square, either passing through or stopping in that square.
- ☐ Lines must start at a black square.
- ☐ Numbers on black squares indicate the total number of white squares entered by lines starting at that square.
- ☐ Lines can only run horizontally and vertically and cannot bend.
- ☐ Lines can't cross, or touch more than one black square.

Re-Thinking
MEDITATION

Some people find it easy to dismiss meditation or breathing exercises as something irrelevant to their lives. But the fact is they can often help, and there is even evidence that meditation can build additional redundancy in the brain, offsetting some of the effects of aging.

Unless you're a saint, you probably start to feel irate or even angry from time to time. Occasionally this is a useful response which encourages you to do the right thing, but it's also often a distraction that merely upsets you without any useful gain. Taking deep breaths can really help here. Firstly, committing to take a moment's pause before acting can in itself make a big difference, but secondly a deep breath naturally calms the body by simulating a period of rest. And several deep breaths have an even more calming effect.

Meditation, or similar activities such as prayer, can be very important periods for your brain. Taking a moment to stop and consider what's going on in your life, or to think without time pressure about a current activity, helps your brain help you. It can also reduce stress levels, help clear your mind before sleep, and help you feel in control again – no one likes that feeling of not having a single moment to themselves for an entire day. Even just five quiet minutes set aside for yourself can make a big difference.

Instructions

☐ Many of us are continually occupied from when we rise until we sleep, and often there is an overlap with phones and devices next to the bed. Try to eliminate that overlap, so your brain can switch off and knows what's expected of it.

☐ If you're religious, try saying a few quiet prayers at a time of day when you ordinarily wouldn't. If you're not, stop and do nothing for a few minutes. You don't have to think about anything; just trying to let your mind go blank is enough. It may take practice!

Week 50 Solutions

Day 1

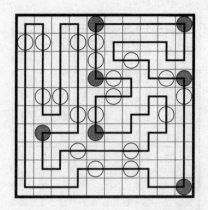

Day 2

SUNS
SONS
CONS
COOS
COOT
FOOT

MOON
MORN
MORE
MARE
RARE
RAGE

Day 3

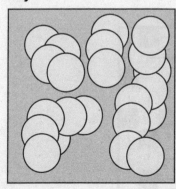

1) 4 chains

2) 22 circles

3) 5 circles

Week 50 Solutions

Day 4

7	4	1	8	6	9	2	5	3
2	9	5	3	7	4	1	8	6
6	3	8	2	1	5	4	9	7
3	7	6	9	4	1	5	2	8
8	5	9	7	3	2	6	4	1
4	1	2	5	8	6	3	7	9
1	8	7	4	2	3	9	6	5
5	6	4	1	9	8	7	3	2
9	2	3	6	5	7	8	1	4

Day 5

Day 6

Week 51

Total Brain Points Available: **185**

Reasoning
HEYAWAKE

This Japanese logic puzzle's name translates as "Divided Rooms".

2		**3**		**3**			
				5			**1**
2		**2**					
				3		**3**	
						2	

Instructions

- ☐ Shade some squares, such that no two shaded squares are adjacent, except diagonally, and all unshaded squares form a single continuous area.
- ☐ Any single horizontal or vertical line of unshaded squares cannot cross more than one bold line.
- ☐ Numbered squares may or may not be shaded, but always give the precise amount of shaded squares in their bold-lined region.

Language
MULTI-ANAGRAM

Can you find the given number of anagrams of each of the following sets of letters? Each anagram must be a standard English word, and it must use *all* of the given letters once each.

5 anagrams:
A E G I L N R T

3 anagrams:
A C E I N N S T

3 anagrams:
E I N P R R S T

Reasoning
BATTLESHIPS

Find the ships in this solo version of the classic two-player game.

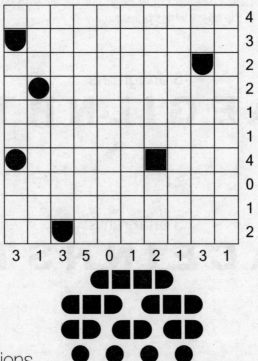

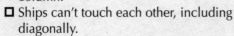

Instructions

☐ Locate the position of each of the listed ships in the grid. Ships are placed horizontally or vertically only.
☐ Numbers around the edge tell you the number of ship segments in each row and column.
☐ Ships can't touch each other, including diagonally.
☐ Some ship segments are already given.

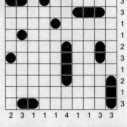

Observation
PHRASEOLOGY

This illustration represents a well-known phrase. Can you work out what it is?

This second illustration also represents a well-known phrase. Can you work out what phrase that is?

1 1 1   other other other
1 1 1   other other other

Language
ARROWWORD

Solve this crossword where the clues are written inside the grid.

At the same time ▼		Ate ▼		Steps down ▼		Persian Gulf state (inits)
Musical drama ▶				▼		Entry permits
She		Low in pitch ▶				▼
⌐▶			Gradually wear away		Hereditary unit	
Transforms		Two-wheeled carriages ▶ ▼			▼	
⌐▶						
Leafs through		Henry VIII's wife, Boleyn ▶				
⌐▶						

Reasoning

TOROIDAL NUMBER LINK

This puzzle allows lines to 'wrap around' from one side of the puzzle to the other!

1				
2	3	2	1	4
		3		
4				

Instructions

☐ Draw a series of separate paths, each connecting a pair of identical numbers, as in the example.

☐ No more than one line can pass through any square, and lines can only travel horizontally or vertically between squares.

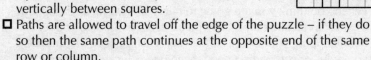

☐ Paths are allowed to travel off the edge of the puzzle – if they do so then the same path continues at the opposite end of the same row or column.

Re-Thinking
THE PLACEBO EFFECT

Having confidence or a real belief in something is very important for your brain. Positive emotions reinforce brain behaviours, just as a treat is used to teach a dog new tricks.

The body is amazingly complex, and it is capable of fighting hard in order to heal itself from many different ailments – although unfortunately, of course, there are also many illnesses beyond its abilities, and no amount of positive thinking will affect these. But many minor ailments, from headaches to some cold symptoms, can sometimes go away faster when you truly believe they will go away. The same also applies to many pain sensations, and in some people the belief of the use of an anaesthetic is in and of itself enough to reduce the perception of pain.

It's for this reason that a whole host of claimed treatments for various ailments will sometimes work perfectly well, despite the treatment itself having no direct effect. The colour of a pill, or the size of it, or the way it's taken influences our brain so we draw inferences about its likely effect. Where our body is capable of creating that effect, such as a more robust immune system response to infection, it often does then occur. Conversely, believing that there is no hope often leads to the brain essentially "giving up", and not using the body's natural resources to their full capacity.

Instructions

- ☐ Belief in yourself and your brain's and your body's amazing abilities is really important. If you've solved even a few of the puzzles in this book then you've shown that you have an incredibly capable brain, and you should never forget it.
- ☐ When you think you are going to fail, you help make it happen. If you start tackling an issue with a negative outlook, you're handicapping your brain. At the very least, believe that maybe if you're lucky you will succeed. Everyone is lucky sometimes.

Week 51 Solutions

Day 1

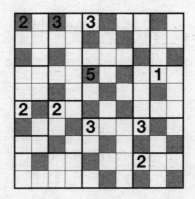

Day 2

ALERTING ALTERING INTEGRAL RELATING
TRIANGLE

ANCIENTS CANNIEST INSTANCE

PRINTERS REPRINTS SPRINTER

Day 3

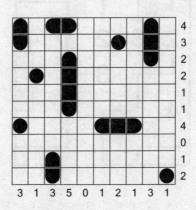

Week 51 Solutions

Day 4

The time of your life

Six of one and half a dozen of the other

Day 5

	T	F		U	
	O	P	E	R	A	
	G		D	E	E	P
H	E	R		S		A
	T		G	I	G	S
C	H	A	N	G	E	S
	E		A	N	N	E
B	R	O	W	S	E	S

Day 6

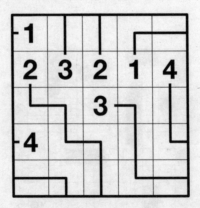

Week 52

Total Brain Points Available: **165**

Reasoning
FOUR-BRIDGE HASHI

This variant of the puzzle allows up to four bridges between islands.

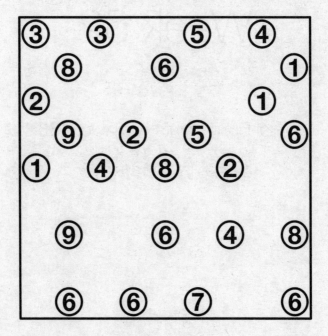

Instructions

☐ Join circled numbers with horizontal or vertical lines.

☐ Each number must have as many lines connected to it as specified by its value.

☐ No more than four lines may join any pair of numbers.

☐ No lines may cross.

☐ The finished layout must allow you to travel from any number to any other number just by following one or more lines.

Language
VOWEL PLAY

All of the vowels have been removed from the following words.
What were the original words? They are all common English words.

VRZLS

MLLNNM

DFG

CDCL

RNNGS

Number Skills
SCALES

Looking at the scales, can you work out how much each shape weighs, in kilograms?

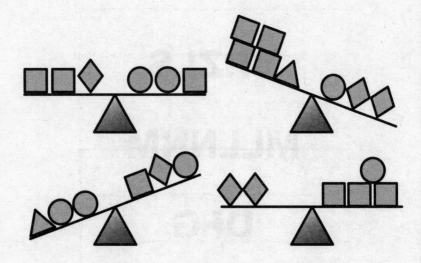

Instructions

- ☐ Assume that the lightest shape weighs the smallest possible whole number of kilograms.
- ☐ Ignore the distance from the fulcrum.
- ☐ As a hint, none of the shapes weighs more than a single-digit number of kilograms.

Reasoning
CALCUDOKU

This is another Latin Square puzzle, but this time the clues come in the form of mathematical constraints.

4+	24×			3−	
	7+		8×	8+	2÷
24×					
3÷	2−	90×		5+	
			2×		6+
5÷		13+			

Instructions

☐ Place the numbers 1 to 6 once each into every row and column of the grid, while obeying the region totals.

☐ The value at the top-left of each bold-lined region must be obtained when all of the numbers in that region have the given operation (+, -, ×, ÷) applied between them. For - and ÷ operations start with the largest number in the region and then subtract or divide by the other numbers.

6× 2	20× 5	4	24× 1	18× 3	6
3	4× 4	1	6	7+ 5	2÷ 2
90× 6	3	5	4	2	1
4− 1	6÷ 6	1− 2	12+ 3	4	5
5	1	3	4− 2	6	1− 4
6× 4	2	6	5÷ 5	1	3

Observation

CUBE COUNT

How many individual cubes have been used to build the structure below? You should assume that all 'hidden' cubes are present, and that it started off as a perfect 6×4×5 arrangement of cubes (right) before any cubes were removed. There are no floating cubes.

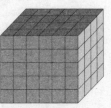

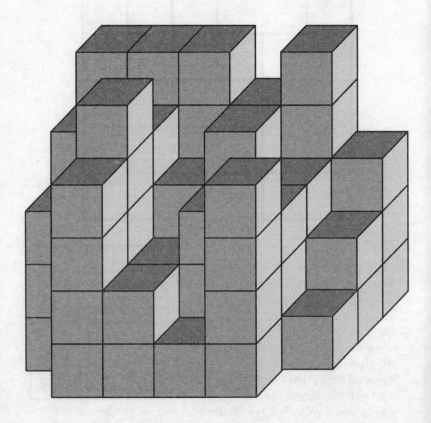

Reasoning
KUROMASU

This Japanese logic puzzle is a good test of your reasoning skills.

	5			9				8	
					12				
		12					4		
		17				16		16	11
10	5		7				9		
		10					6		
			11						
	3				5			5	

Instructions

- ☐ Shade in some squares, so that each number in the grid indicates the number of unshaded squares that can be seen from that square in the same row and column, including the square itself. Counting stops when you reach a shaded square.

- ☐ No square with a number in can be shaded.
- ☐ Shaded squares cannot touch, except diagonally.
- ☐ All unshaded squares must form a single continuous area, so you can move left/right/up/down from one unshaded square to another to reach any other unshaded square.

Re-Thinking
EXPLORE AND HAVE FUN

If you take away just one thing from this year of brain training activities, remember that looking after your brain is all about presenting it with as much variety as possible. And if you can, make that variety fun. A happy brain is a brain that works well.

Smile. Your brain associates smiling with happiness, and, remarkably, the connection is so strong in your mind that it works the other way too. Just the very act of smiling can make you happier!

Try to feel good about yourself. Do little acts of selflessness, if you can, such as donating to charity or helping out a friend. If you feel good about yourself, you'll be healthier and your brain will work better.

Sit up straight when you're working – your brain associates your posture with how serious you're being. Tell it you're serious about your work and you might even start feeling more alert.

Act as if you're happy, and over time you'll actually *be* happier. Studies have shown that one begets the other.

Find puzzles or problems to challenge you. There are lots to be found online, and countless puzzle books in bookstores.

Instructions

☐ If you enjoyed this book, try *The Mammoth Book of Fun Brain Training*, by the same author. It's also available in colour ebook format with revised puzzles that don't require you to write in the book to solve them! See pages 541 and 543 for more information.

☐ Join the author's brain training website, www.BrainedUp.com – you'll find a set of personalized daily challenges, and the chance to follow a range of other brain-enriching activities.

☐ Look for the fun in life's challenges, even if it's hard to find!

Week 52 Solutions

Day 1

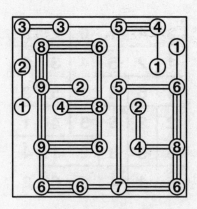

Day 2

OVERZEALOUS

MILLENNIUM

DEFOG

CODICIL

EARNINGS

Day 3

The square weighs 3kg

The circle weighs 5kg

The triangle weighs 6kg

The diamond weighs 7kg

Week 52 Solutions

Day 4

3 (4+)	4 (24×)	1	6	2 (3−)	5
1	2 (7+)	5	4 (8×)	3 (8+)	6 (2÷)
4 (24×)	6	2	1	5	3
2 (3÷)	3 (2−)	6 (90×)	5	4 (5+)	1
6	5	3	2 (2×)	1	4 (6+)
5 (5÷)	1	4 (13+)	3	6	2

Day 5

Total cubes = 75

Counting the top layer as level 1, this is made up of:
Level 1 cubes = 5
Level 2 cubes = 11
Level 3 cubes = 17
Level 4 cubes = 20
Level 4 cubes = 22

Day 6

	5			9				8	
					12				
		12					4		
		17				16		16	11
10	5		7				9		
		10					6		
				11					
	3				5			5	

Final Brain Rank

Brain Rankings

POINTS TO RANKS

At the end of each week there is a box in which to write your current brain ranking.

These brain rankings help you to keep track of the progress and the effort you've put into your brain training routine so far. They also provide an incentive to keep pushing for the next level. There is, however, no universal conversion between points and ability, so the precise wording of these rankings is just for your enjoyment and doesn't represent a precise scientific assessment of your skills. Increasing your brain points is an excellent aim, however, and the more you can push for as many points as possible on every task, the better you'll be looking after your brain.

There are a total of 8,615 points to be won across the entire book. If you can reach a total of 5,000 then you have truly done incredibly well, and you are certainly an above-average solver! You'll also have done your brain the world of good, so you should take real pride in the 'BRAINED UP!' epithet.

Turn the page for the full ranking chart. When you reach or exceed the total points shown in the column on the left, award yourself the rank shown in the column on the right.

Brain Rankings

CONVERSION CHART

See the previous page for an explanation of this table.

0	Just started
50	Beginner
100	Getting going
175	Making progress
250	Learner
325	No longer a novice
450	Trainee
600	Apprentice
750	Brain cadet
900	Recruit
1000	In the door
1250	In the brain club
1500	On your way up
1750	Pumping brain
2000	Doing well
2250	Sailing fair
2500	In control
2750	On track
3000	Quick-witted

Brain Rankings

CONVERSION CHART

Reaching 5000 points is an amazing achievement. The rest is for fun!

3250	Sharp as a tack
3500	Extra-smart
3750	Powered up
4000	High achiever
4250	Mega achiever
4500	Ready to celebrate
4750	Verging on victory
5000	**BRAINED UP!**
5250	Exceptional
5500	Phenomenal
5750	Unequalled
6000	Prodigious
6250	One in a thousand
6500	Outstanding
6750	Breathtakingly good
7000	One in ten thousand
7500	Super-size-brained
8000	Ultra-mega-brained
8500	Impossibly perfect

Notes

Use these pages to keep track of your progress with the various Re-Thinking tasks throughout the book.

Notes

Notes

Notes

Notes

Notes

Notes

By The Same Author

The Mammoth Book of Fun Brain Training
By Dr Gareth Moore

ebook ISBN: 978-1-47211-183-8

A one-of-a-kind full-colour brain training ebook with brand new content

Rewritten from cover to cover, a third of the original printed book's content has been modified or replaced so that the book can be used without requiring you to write on the page. The original instructions have additionally been rewritten for ebook use.

Bonus downloadable content is also included, with live links in the book that take you to additional creative tasks derived from those in the original edition of the book.

Available now in iPad iBooks, for all colour Kindle readers, and more

A few minutes a day of FUN BRAIN TRAINING can bring lasting improvement to:

Memory, Logic and Reasoning
Visual and Spatial Awareness
Word and Language Skills
Number Skills

Visit www.constablerobinson.com or www.runningpress.com for more information.

The Mammoth Book of Brain Workouts
By Gareth Moore

UK ISBN: 978-1-84529-805-0
US ISBN: 978-0-7624-3375-9

A sharper, smarter brain in just 31 days

Have you ever gone into a room and forgotten why you are there? The synaptic connections between neurons in your brain degenerate with lack of use. So you need to exercise it – and ALL of it, not just a small part. Keep your brain in tip-top condition, and the rest will follow!

This brilliant new puzzle collection has been specially formulated to challenge, stimulate and train all the key different parts of your brain. It's the most complete brain workout programme available, with a whole month's supply of workouts – comprising over 1,000 individual puzzles and exercises.

Each daily workout contains a carefully balanced mixture of puzzles designed to improve your problem solving, to stimulate your creativity, to enhance your concentration, to improve your memory, and to boost your mind power. They'll leave you feeling refreshed and alive.

Visit www.constablerobinson.com or www.runningpress.com for more information.

By The Same Author

The Mammoth Book of Fun Brain Training
By Dr Gareth Moore

UK ISBN: 978-1-84901-434-2
US ISBN: 978-0-7624-4093-1

A fun and easy way to a better and brighter you!

In full colour throughout, this is the truly fun way to a fitter brain. Many brain-training programmes set tasks which are far from enjoyable, such as completing page after page of mathematical equations or trying to recall long lists of objects. The Mammoth Book of Fun Brain Training changes all that with an approach which is all about FUN! There are also "creative" puzzles, often with a twist – both more entertaining and more effective as they call on multiple skills simultaneously.

Only a few minutes of FUN BRAIN TRAINING can bring LASTING IMPROVEMENT to your:

Memory, Logic and Reasoning
Visual and Spatial Awareness
Word and Language Skills
Number Skills

Visit www.constablerobinson.com or www.runningpress.com for more information.

By The Same Author

The Mammoth Book of New Sudoku
By Dr Gareth Moore

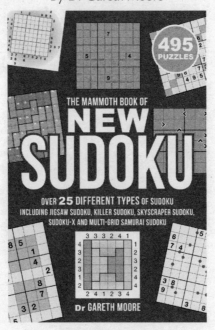

UK ISBN: 978-1-47210-022-1
US ISBN: 978-0-7624-4936-1

Much more than just a puzzle book

A comprehensive collection featuring every significant variant ever created

Over **25** major Sudoku types

Nearly **150** different variants

Almost **500** puzzles, all created especially for this book, including jigsaw sudoku, killer sudoku and multi-grid samurai sudoku

No other collection of Sudoku comes close. This is without doubt the most definitive volume of sudoku variants ever compiled, with full instructions and solutions included

Visit www.constablerobinson.com or www.runningpress.com for more information